PIANO/VOCAL SELECTIONS

Avenue Q - The Musical

Kevin McCollum   Robyn Goodman   Jeffrey Seller
Vineyard Theatre   and   The New Group
present

Music and Lyrics by
Robert Lopez and Jeff Marx

Book by
Jeff Whitty

Based on an Original Concept by
Robert Lopez and Jeff Marx

with
**Jennifer Barnhart, Natalie Venetia Belcon, Stephanie D'Abruzzo,
Jordan Gelber, Ann Harada, Rick Lyon, John Tartaglia**

Puppets Conceived and Designed by
Rick Lyon

Set Design	Costume Design	Lighting Design	Sound Design
Anna Louizos	**Mirena Rada**	**Howell Binkley**	**Acme Sound Partners**

Animation Design	Music Director & Incidental Music	Music Coordinator	Casting
Robert Lopez	**Gary Adler**	**Michael Keller**	**Cindy Tolan**

Technical Supervisor	Press Representative	Marketing
Brian Lynch	**Sam Rudy Media Relations**	**TMG-The Marketing Group**

General Manager	Production Stage Manager	Associate Producers
John Corker	**Evan Ensign**	**Sonny Everett Walter Grossman Mort Swinsky**

Music Supervision, Arrangement
and Orchestrations by
Stephen Oremus

Choreographer
Ken Roberson

Directed by
Jason Moore

Avenue Q was supported by a residency and public staged reading at the
2002 O'Neill Music Theatre Conference of the Eugene O'Neill Theater Center, Waterford, CT

Interior Photos by Carol Rosegg
Photo of Jeff Marx & Robert Lopez by Ben Strothmann

The composers wish to thank Paul Ford, Gary Adler, Harris Doran, Helene Blue, and Maxyne Lang for their gracious
assistance, and Mark Carlstein and the entire Hal Leonard team for their diligent efforts in preparing this book.

To contact the authors (particularly to report any inadvertent errors in this book), please visit us at www.lopezmarx.com.
Any corrections will be posted and periodically updated at that site.

ISBN 0-634-07919-0

**HAL•LEONARD®
CORPORATION**

7777 W. BLUEMOUND RD. P.O. BOX 13819 MILWAUKEE, WI 53213

In Australia Contact:
Hal Leonard Australia Pty. Ltd.
22 Taunton Drive P.O. Box 5130
Cheltenham East, 3192 Victoria, Australia
Email: ausadmin@halleonard.com

Visit Hal Leonard Online at
www.halleonard.com

Avenue Q is Robert Lopez and Jeff Marx's first Broadway show.

Jeff Marx & Robert Lopez

They began writing it in the BMI Lehman Engel Musical Theater Workshop in 1999, thinking it would be a great TV series. Once they had a handful of songs and a rough "pilot episode" ready, they presented it in a borrowed theater in the basement of a church. At that very first reading, major theater producers (responsible for *Rent*, *De La Guarda*, *Metamorphoses*, *Bat Boy*, and others) approached them and asked if they would be interested in developing *Avenue Q* not as a TV show, but as a stage musical. With little hesitation, they answered, "okay!" Dozens of drafts and developmental readings later, *Avenue Q* was produced Off-Broadway at the Vineyard Theatre, where it won critical acclaim and the 2003 Lucille Lortel Award for Best Musical. The reception was so great that the producers decided to move the show to Broadway! It opened on Broadway at the John Golden Theater on July 31, 2003. It won three 2004 Tony Awards: Best Original Score, Best Book of a Musical, and the top prize, Best Musical.

Bobby and Jeff's previous works include a yet-to-be-produced Muppet movie called *Kermit, Prince of Denmark* (which received the coveted Kleban Award), two children's musicals commissioned by Theatreworks/USA, and several songs for The Disney Channel's series *The Book of Pooh* and *Bear and the Big Blue House*.

Bobby and Jeff are extremely grateful for all the contributions of their wonderfully talented collaborators, who helped make *Avenue Q* possible. They also would like to acknowledge and thank those artists who have provided them with so much inspiration: Jeff Moss, Joe Raposo, The Beatles, Stephen Sondheim, Paul Williams, Billy Joel, Barry Manilow, John Kander and Fred Ebb, Stephen Trask and John Cameron Mitchell, Trey Parker and Matt Stone and Marc Shaiman. And of course, Frank Oz and Jim Henson.

Bobby earned a B.A. in English at Yale. Jeff has a B.F.A. in Musical Theater from the University of Michigan and a J.D. from Cardozo Law School. They both wish they could go back to college. Life was so simple back then.

See www.lopezmarx.com for the latest news and updates.

Order Avenue Q merchandise (posters, t-shirts, caps, mouse pads, mugs, karaoke albums, even a souvenir booklet containing a CD of a song which was cut from the show!) at www.AvenueQstuff.com

THE AVENUE Q THEME

from the Broadway Musical AVENUE Q

Music and Lyrics by ROBERT LOPEZ
and JEFF MARX

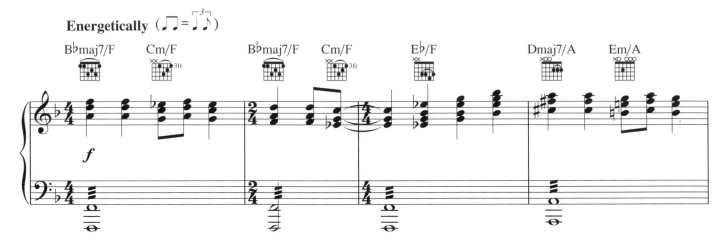

GIRLS: Ba da ba _____

GUYS: Do do do _____ do do do _

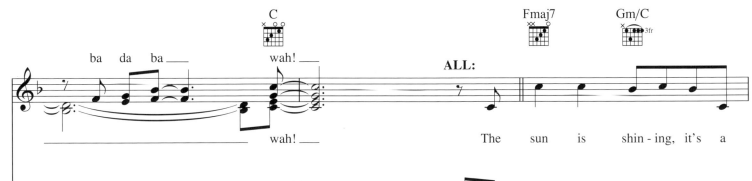

ba da ba _____ wah! _____ ALL:

_____ wah! The sun is shin-ing, it's a

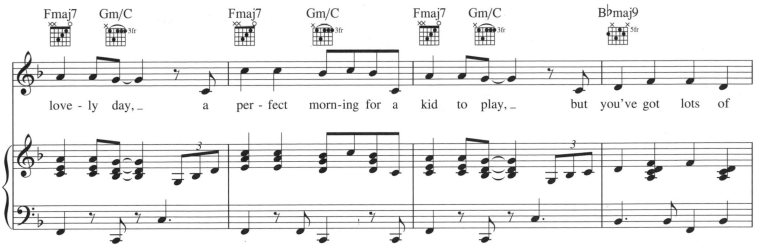

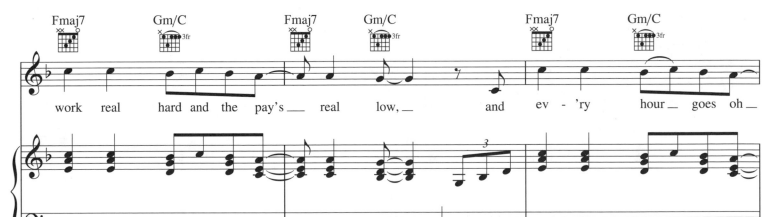

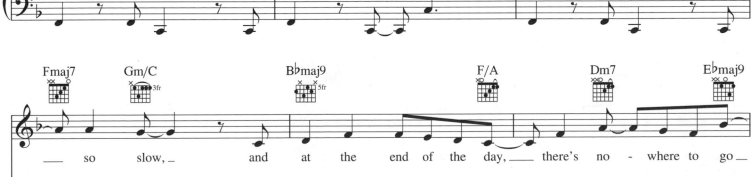

WHAT DO YOU DO WITH A B.A. IN ENGLISH

from the Broadway Musical AVENUE Q

Music and Lyrics by ROBERT LOPEZ
and JEFF MARX

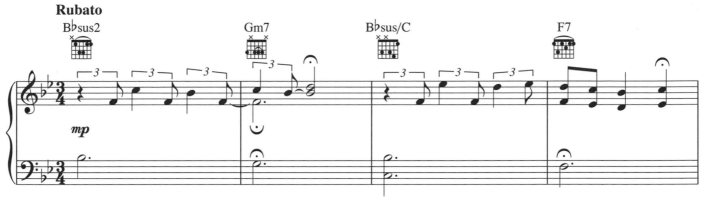

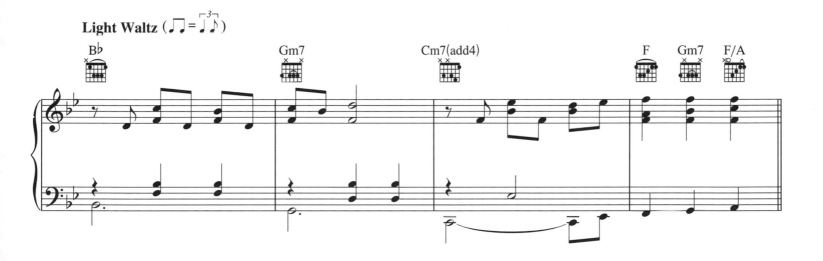

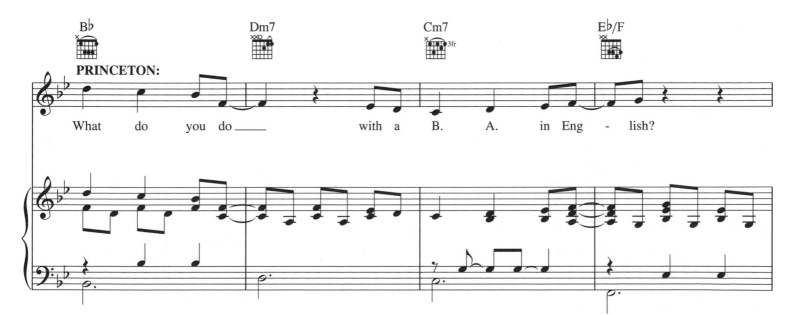

PRINCETON:

What do you do ___ with a B. A. in Eng - lish?

What is my life ___ going to be?

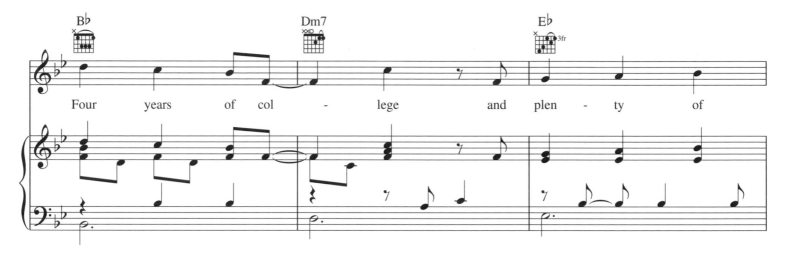

Four years of col - lege and plen - ty of

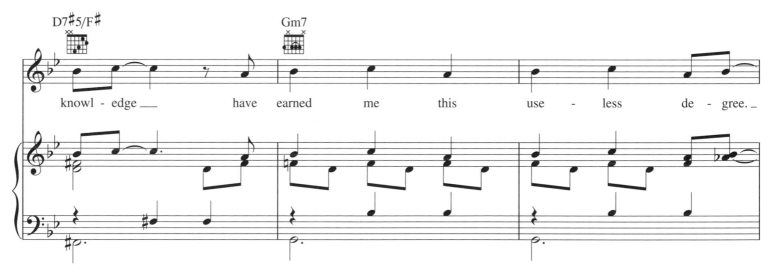

knowl - edge ___ have earned me this use - less de - gree. ___

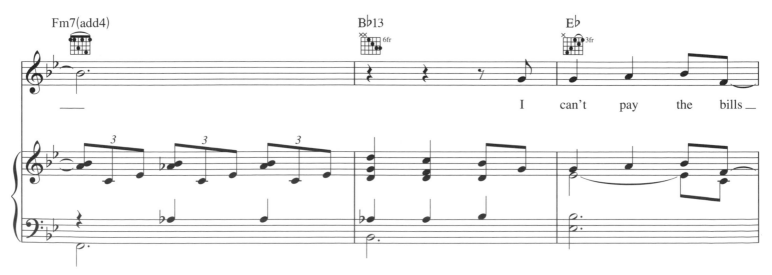

I can't pay the bills ___

IT SUCKS TO BE ME

from the Broadway Musical AVENUE Q

Music and Lyrics by ROBERT LOPEZ
and JEFF MARX

BRIAN: When I was lit-tle, I thought I would be... KATE: What?

BRIAN: a big co-me-di-an on late night T V.

But now I'm thir-ty-two ___ and as you can see, ___ I'm not.

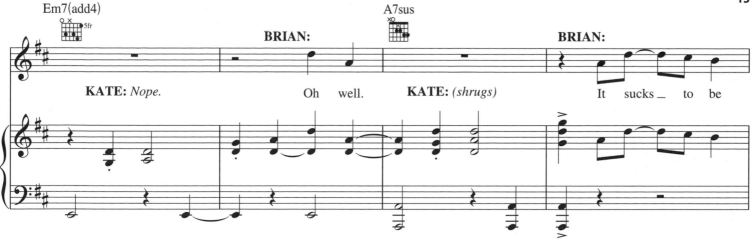

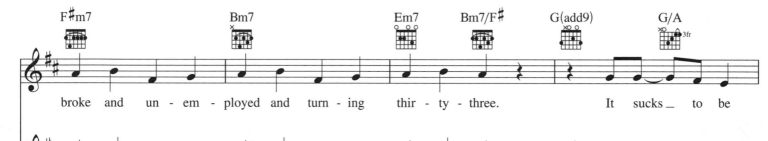

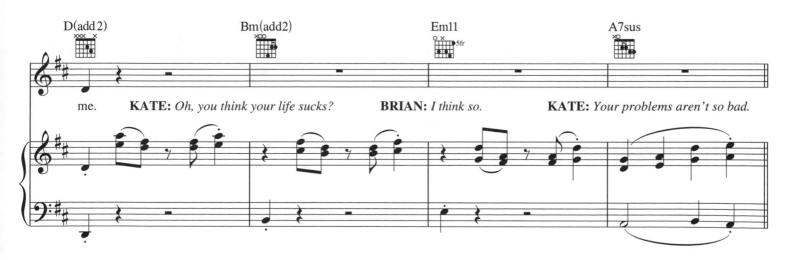

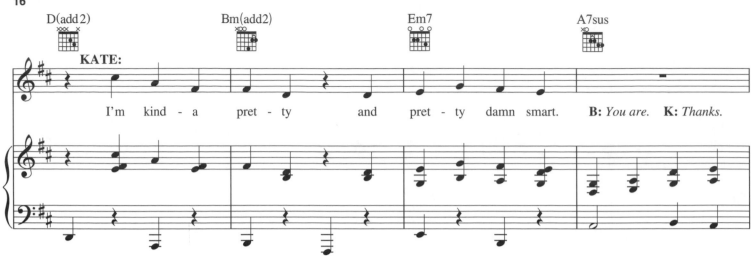

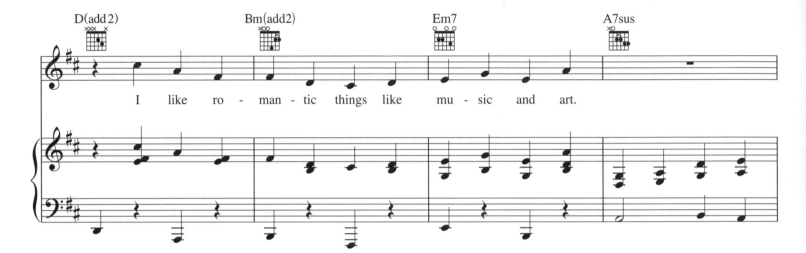

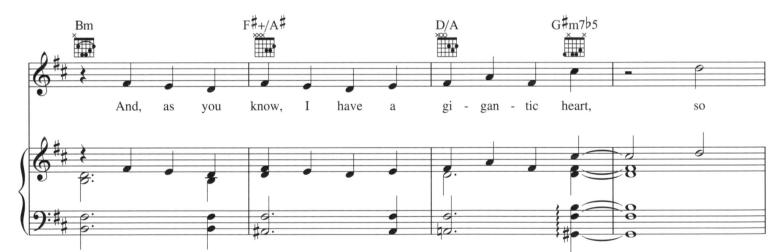

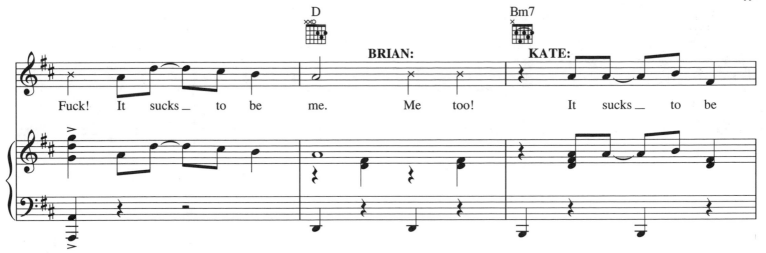

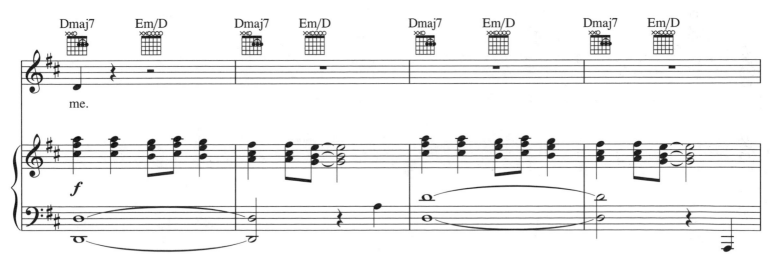

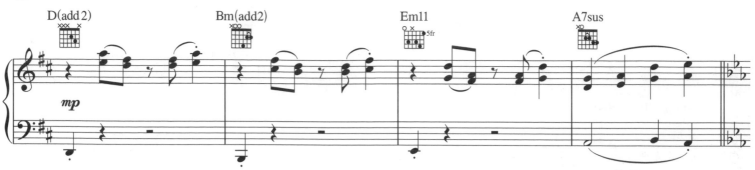

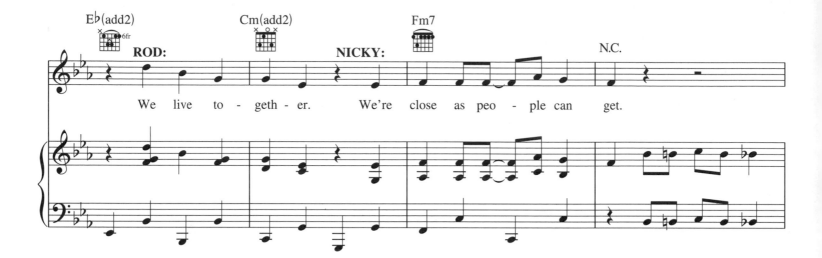

We live to - geth - er. We're close as peo - ple can get.

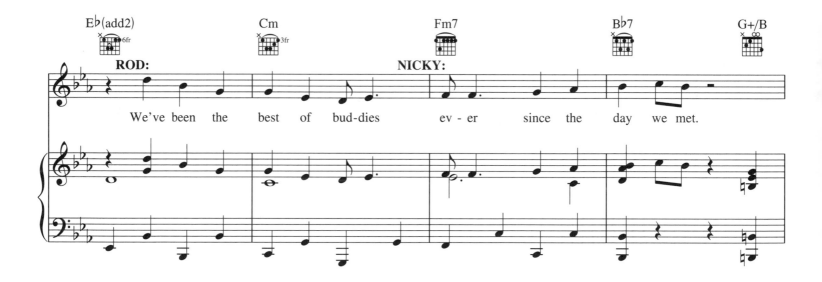

We've been the best of bud-dies ev - er since the day we met.

So he knows lots of ways to make me real - ly up - set. Oh,

ev - 'ry day is an ag - gra - va - tion. Come on, that's an ex - ag - ger - a - tion!

ROD: You leave your clothes out. You put your feet__ on my chair. Oh yeah?

NICKY: You do such a - nal things, like i - ron - ing your un - der - wear.__

ROD: You make that ver - y small a - part - ment we share ____ a

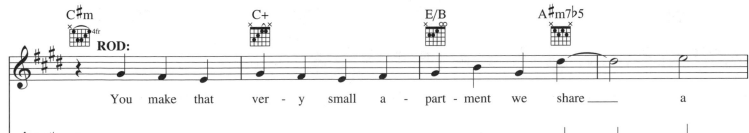

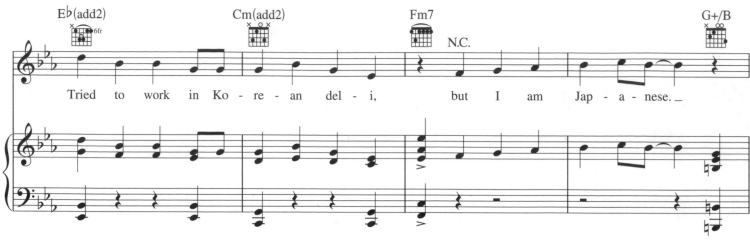

Tried to work in Ko-re-an del-i, but I am Jap-a-nese.

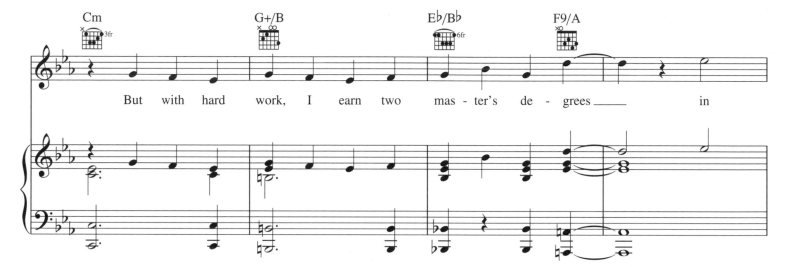

But with hard work, I earn two mas-ter's de-grees _____ in

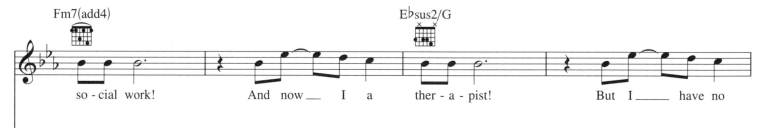

so-cial work! And now __ I a ther-a-pist! But I____ have no

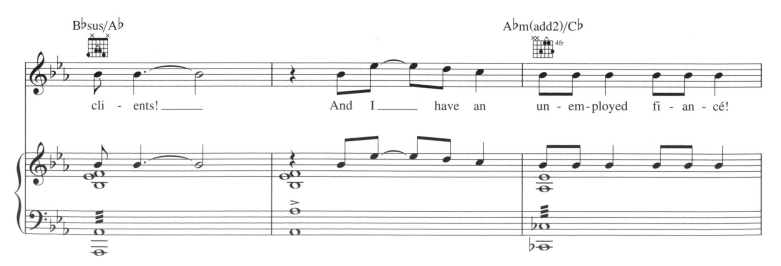

cli - ents! _____ And I____ have an un-em-ployed fi-an-cé!

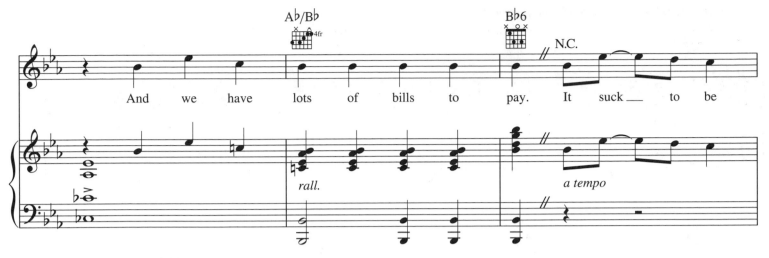

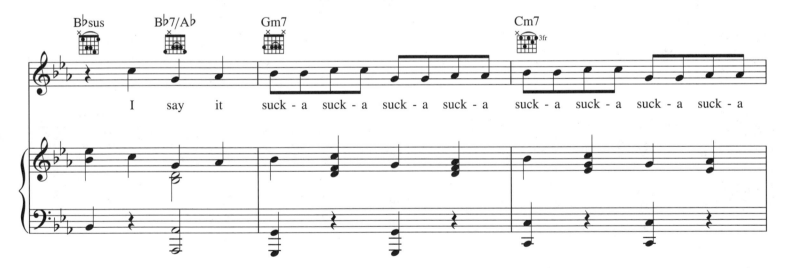

24

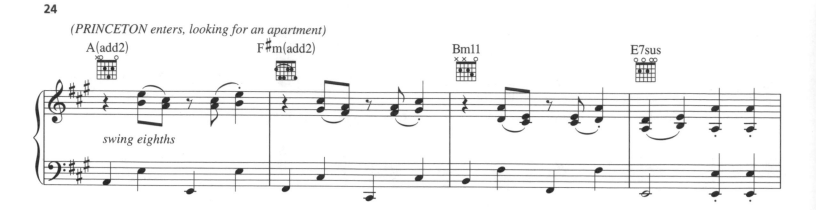

(*PRINCETON enters, looking for an apartment*)

swing eighths

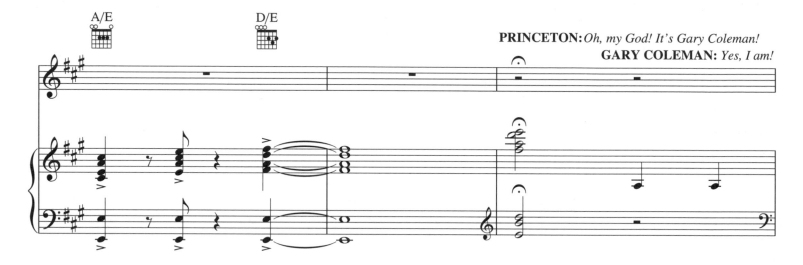

PRINCETON: *Oh, my God! It's Gary Coleman!*
GARY COLEMAN: *Yes, I am!*

Funky

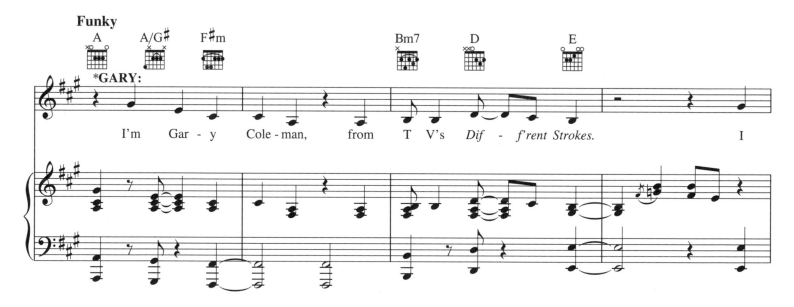

*GARY:

I'm Gar - y Cole - man, from T V's *Dif - f'rent Strokes.* I

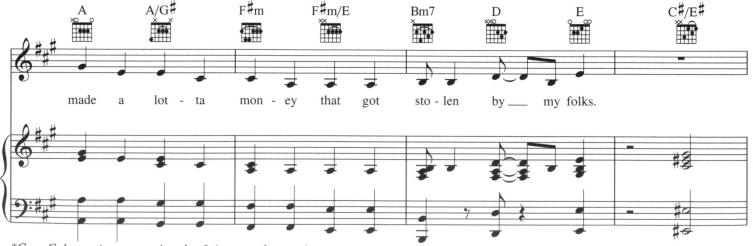

made a lot - ta mon - ey that got sto - len by ___ my folks.

*Gary Coleman is a woman's role. It is sung where written.

Now I'm broke, and I'm the butt of ev-'ry-one's jokes, ___ but I'm

here, *The superintendent!* on Av - e - nue Q!

ALL (except GARY):
It sucks ___ to be

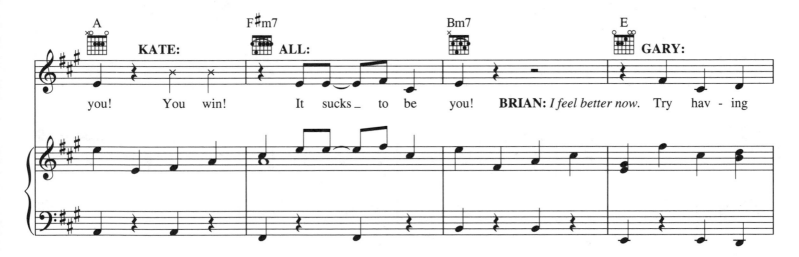

KATE:
you! You win!
ALL:
It sucks ___ to be you!
GARY:
BRIAN: *I feel better now.* Try hav - ing

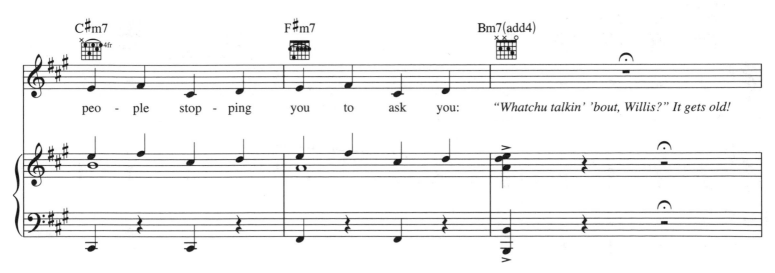

peo - ple stop - ping you to ask you: *"Whatchu talkin' 'bout, Willis?" It gets old!*

live on Av - e - nue Q! _____ Our friends do too! __

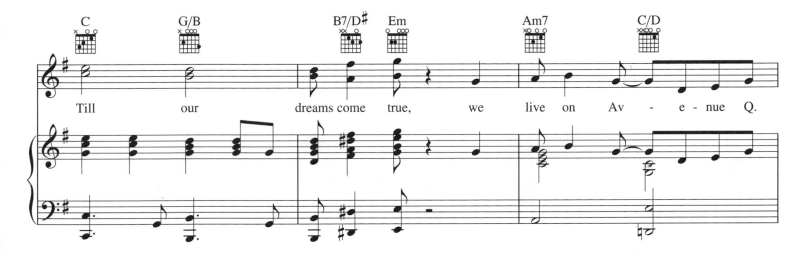

Till our dreams come true, we live on Av - e - nue Q.

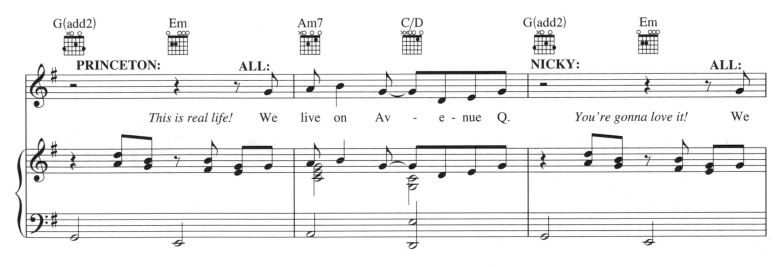

PRINCETON: **ALL:** **NICKY:** **ALL:**

This is real life! We live on Av - e - nue Q. *You're gonna love it!* We

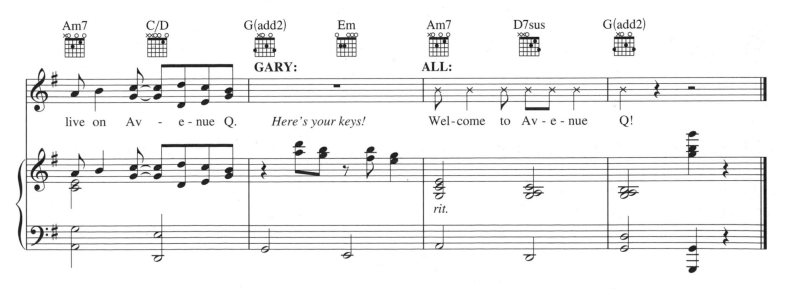

GARY: **ALL:**

live on Av - e - nue Q. *Here's your keys!* Wel - come to Av - e - nue Q!

IF YOU WERE GAY

from the Broadway Musical AVENUE Q

Music and Lyrics by ROBERT LOPEZ
and JEFF MARX

30

hap - py _____ just be - ing with you. **ROD:** *High Button Shoes,*

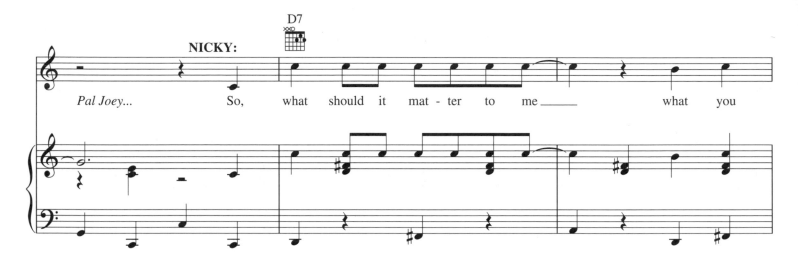

Pal Joey... So, what should it mat - ter to me ____ what you

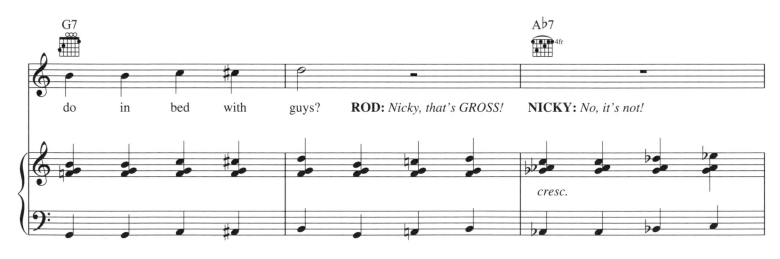

do in bed with guys? **ROD:** *Nicky, that's GROSS!* **NICKY:** *No, it's not!*

If you were gay, I'd shout hoo -

ray! **ROD:** *I am not listening!* **NICKY:** And here I'd stay... **ROD:** *La, la, la, la, la!*

accel. poco a poco

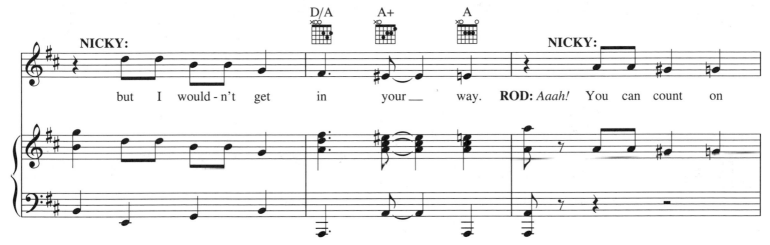

NICKY: but I would-n't get in your ___ way. **ROD:** *Aaah!* **NICKY:** You can count on

me to al - ways be

Faster

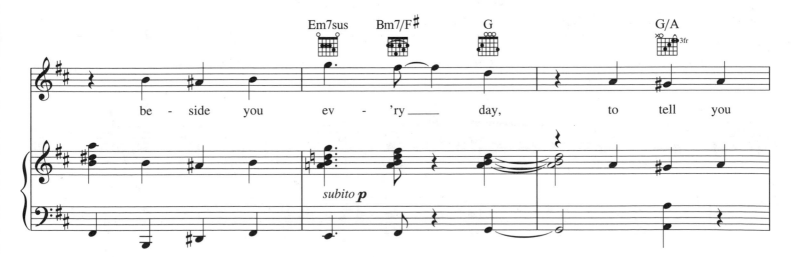

be - side you ev - 'ry ___ day, to tell you

subito **p**

it's o - kay, you were just born that ___ way,

and as they say, it's in your D. N. A., you're

gay! _____ *I'M NOT GAY!!!*

ROD: **NICKY:**

(If you were gay!)

PURPOSE
from the Broadway Musical AVENUE Q

Music and Lyrics by ROBERT LOPEZ
and JEFF MARX

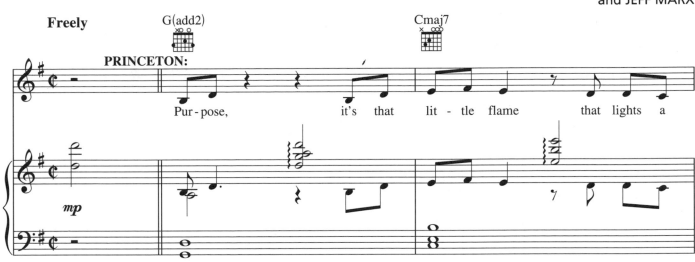

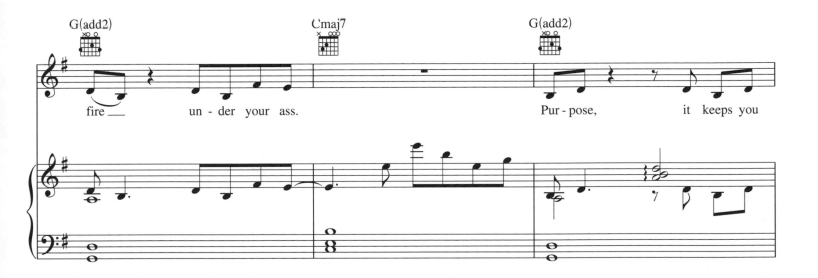

Tempo di "Huey Lewis" (Shuffle)

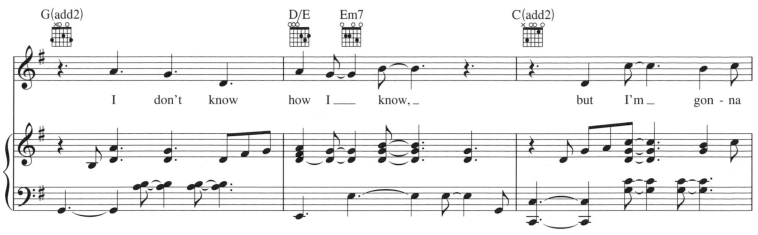

I don't know how I ___ know, ___ but I'm ___ gon - na

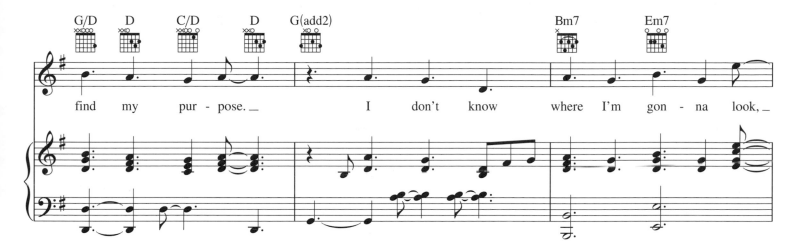

find my pur - pose. ___ I don't know where I'm gon - na look, ___

Half-time feel

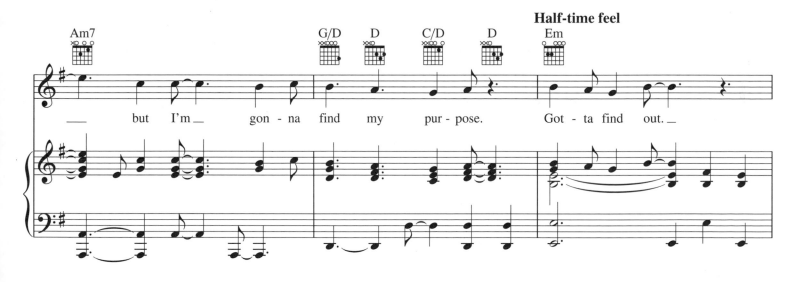

___ but I'm ___ gon - na find my pur - pose. Got - ta find out. ___

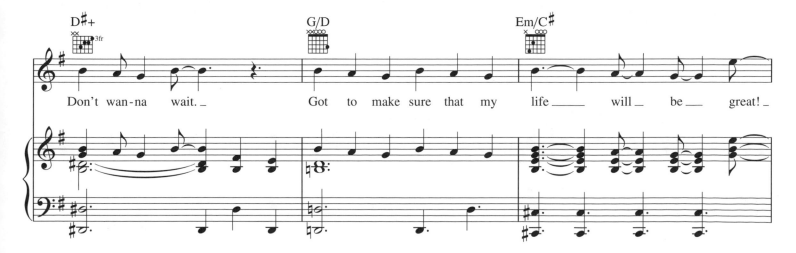

Don't wan - na wait. ___ Got to make sure that my life ___ will ___ be ___ great! ___

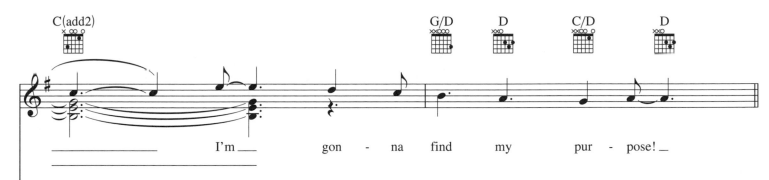

Shuffle feel

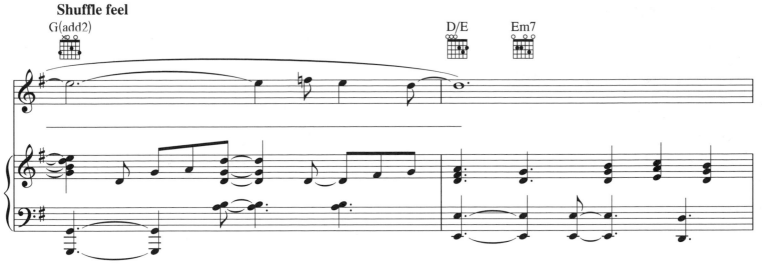

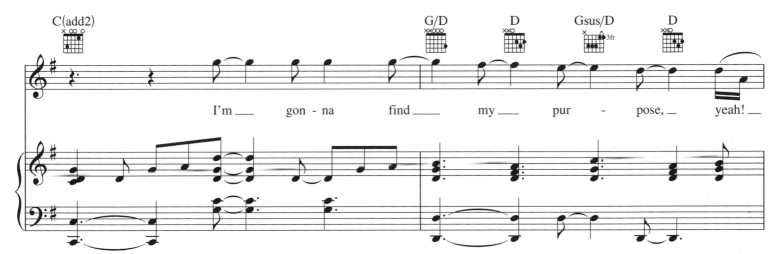

I'm __ gon - na find __ my __ pur - pose, __ yeah! __

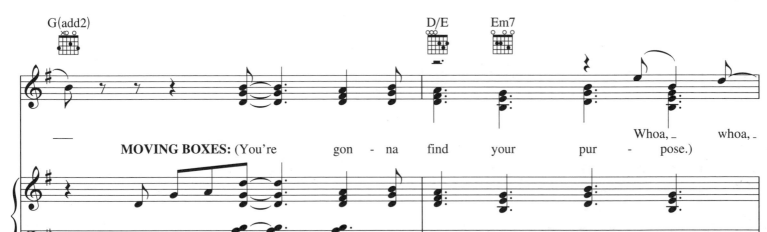

__ **MOVING BOXES:** (You're gon - na find your pur - pose.) Whoa, __ whoa, __

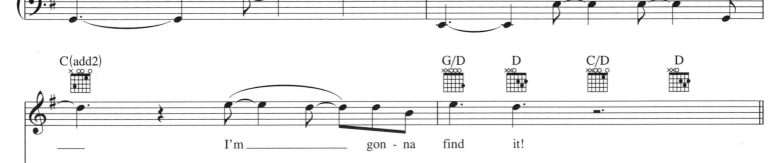

__ I'm _____ gon - na find it!

Half-time feel

What will it be? Where will __ it be? My

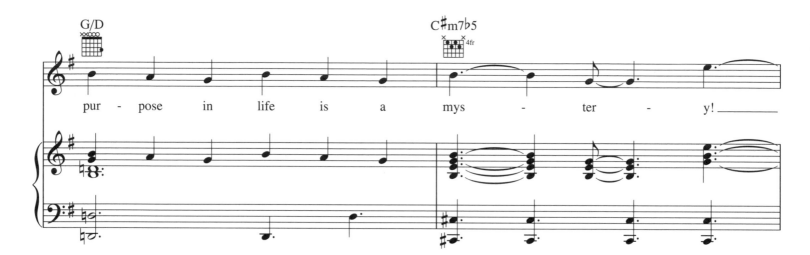

pur - pose in life is a mys - ter - y! _____

Shuffle feel

__ Got - ta find __ my pur - pose. __

Got - ta find __ me! __

(You're __ gon - na find your pur - pose!)

Whoa, __ whoa, __

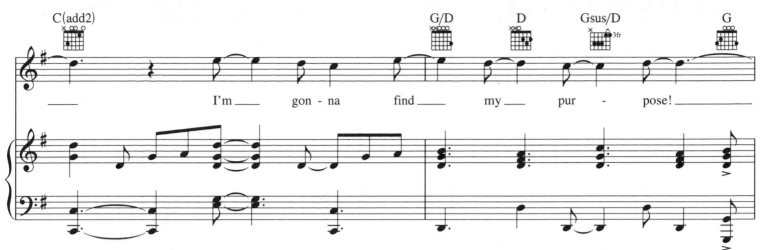

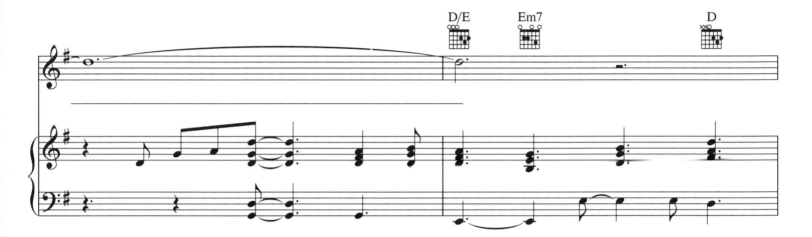

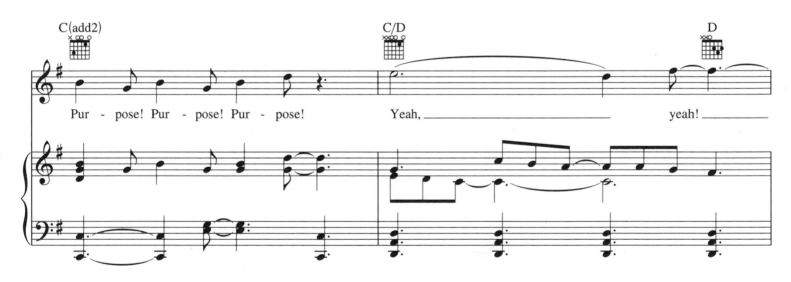

EVERYONE'S A LITTLE BIT RACIST

from the Broadway Musical AVENUE Q

Music and Lyrics by ROBERT LOPEZ
and JEFF MARX

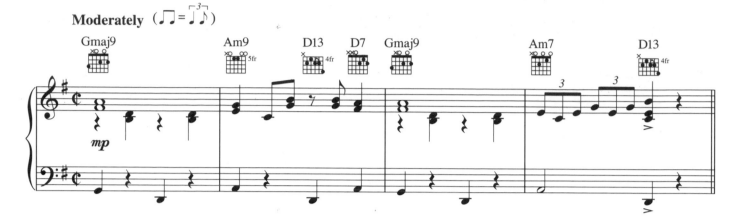

PRINCETON:
You're a lit - tle bit rac - ist.

KATE:
Well, you're a lit - tle bit

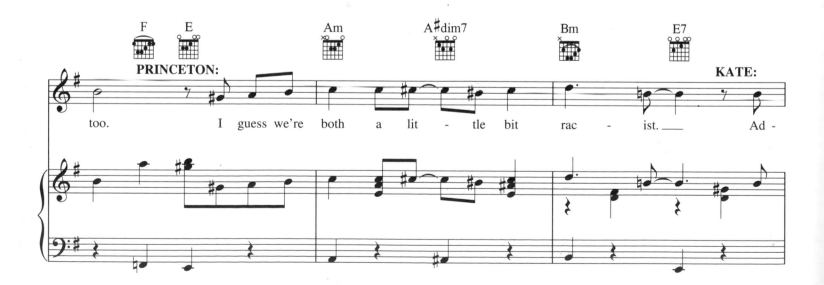

PRINCETON:
too.   I guess we're both a lit - tle bit rac - ist. ___

KATE:
Ad -

For more info about *Avenue Q*, visit www.AvenueQ.com

KATE: You're a lit-tle bit rac-ist. GARY: Well, you're a lit-tle bit,

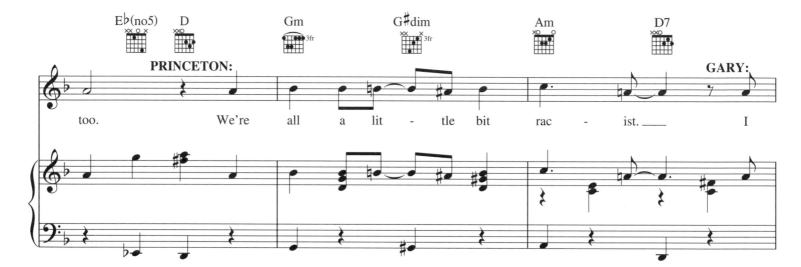

too. PRINCETON: We're all a lit-tle bit rac-ist. ___ GARY: I

think that I would have to a-gree with you. KATE & PRINCETON: We're glad you do. ___ GARY: It's

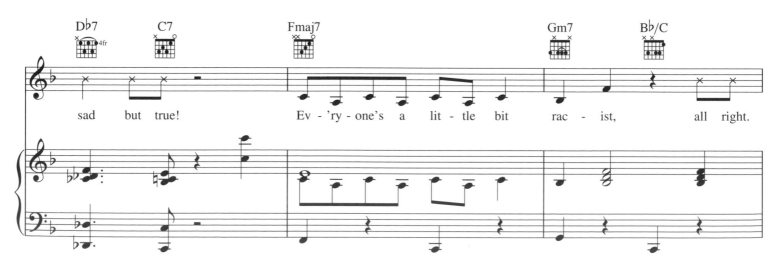

sad but true! Ev-'ry-one's a lit-tle bit rac-ist, all right.

CHRISTMAS EVE: *BLIAN! You come back here!*
You take out lecycuraburs!
PRINCETON: *What's that mean?*
BRIAN: *Ugh! Recyclables.*
(everyone laughs)

BRIAN: *Don't laugh at her! How many languages do you speak?*
KATE: *Oh, come off it, Brian!*

KATE: Ev - 'ry - one's a lit - tle bit rac - ist. I'm not. Oh, no?

BRIAN: Nope. How man - y O - ri - en - tal wives have you

CHRISTMAS EVE: got? What?! BLI - AN!

PRINCETON: Bri - an, bud - dy,

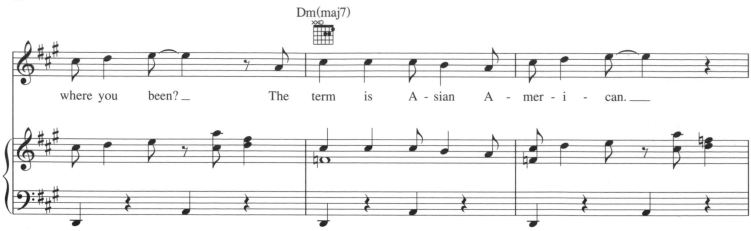

where you been? __ The term is A - sian A - mer - i - can. __

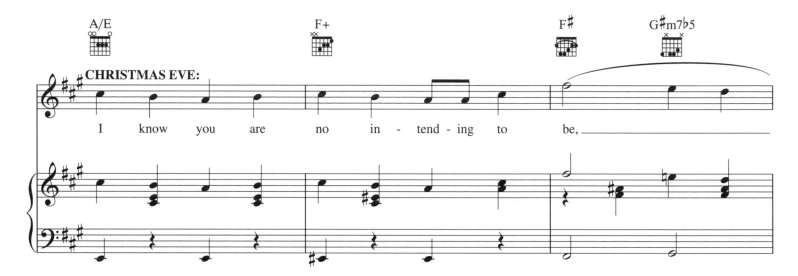

CHRISTMAS EVE:

I know you are no in - tend - ing to be, _____

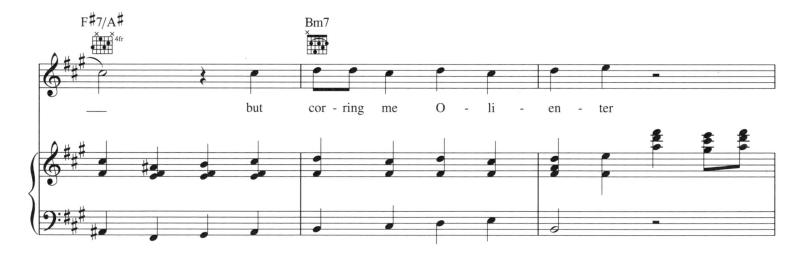

__ but cor - ring me O - li - en - ter

of - fen - sive to me. **BRIAN:** *I'm sorry, honey.*
I love you. **CHRISTMAS EVE:** *And I love you.*

BRIAN: *But you're racist, too.* CHRISTMAS EVE: *Yes, I know.* The Jews have all ___ the

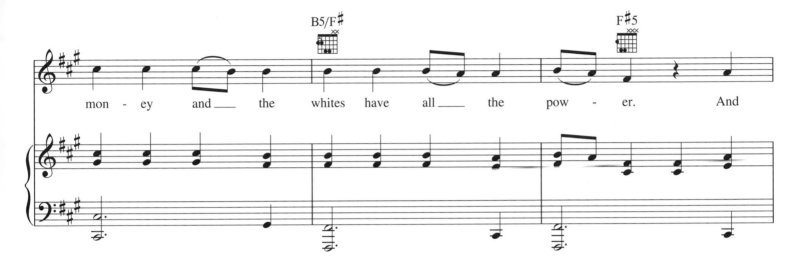

mon - ey and ___ the whites have all ___ the pow - er. And

I'm al - ways in tax - i cab with dli - ver who no

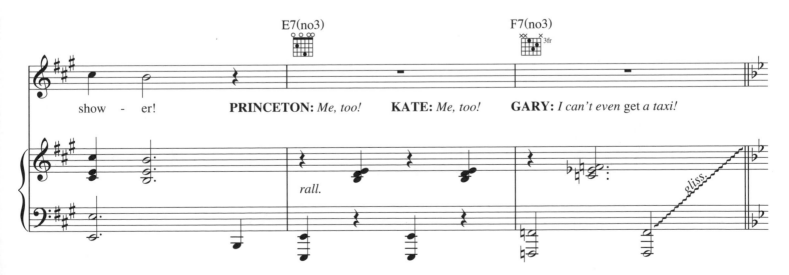

show - er! PRINCETON: *Me, too!* KATE: *Me, too!* GARY: *I can't even get a taxi!*

Broader

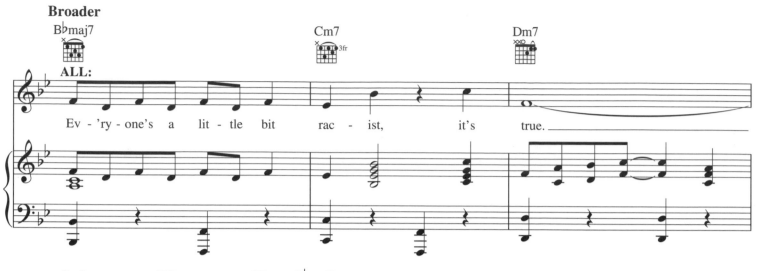

ALL:

Ev - 'ry - one's a lit - tle bit rac - ist, it's true. ____

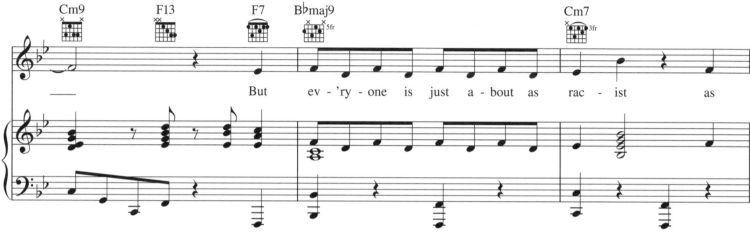

____ But ev - 'ry - one is just a - bout as rac - ist as

Kick-line tempo

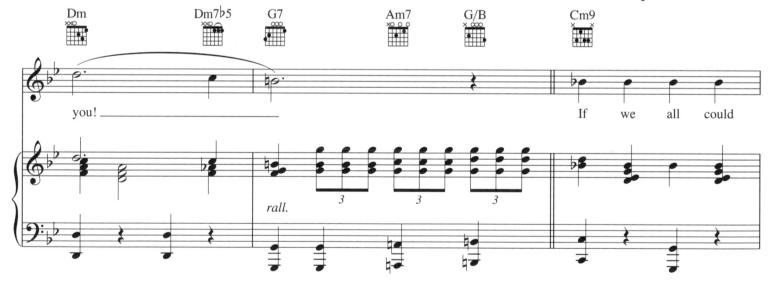

you! ____ If we all could

rall. 3 3 3

just ad - mit that we are rac - ist a lit - tle bit, and

THE INTERNET IS FOR PORN

from the Broadway Musical AVENUE Q

Music and Lyrics by ROBERT LOPEZ
and JEFF MARX

Prissy Sonata, quite fast

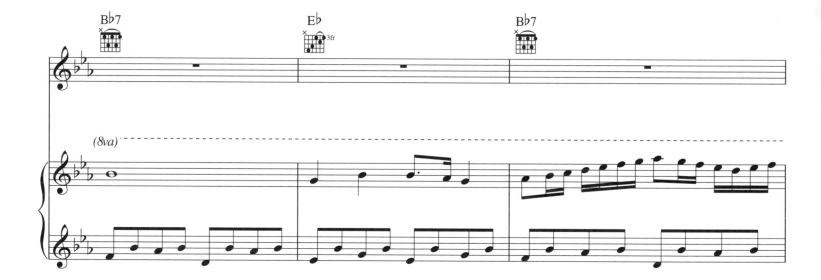

TREKKIE MONSTER: **KATE:**

real - ly, real - ly great. (For porn!) I
new tech - nol - o - gy, (For porn. Oop!) which

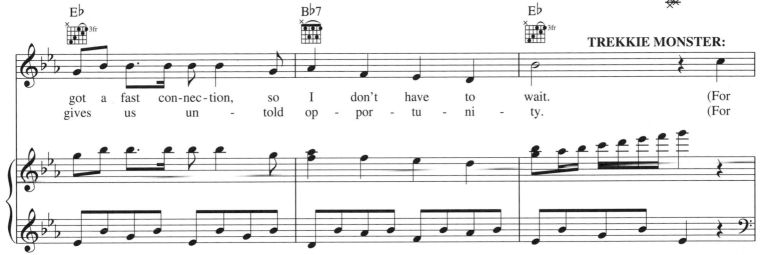

TREKKIE MONSTER:

got a fast con-nec-tion, so I don't have to wait. (For
gives us un - told op - por - tu - ni - ty. (For

KATE: **TREKKIE:**   **KATE:**

porn!) There's al - ways some new site. (For porn!) I
porn. Oops, sorry!) Right from your own desk - top (For p—.) you can

TREKKIE: **KATE:**

browse all day and night. (For porn!) It's like I'm surf - ing
re - search, browse, and shop, (————.) un - til you've had e -

MIX TAPE
from the Broadway Musical AVENUE Q

Music and Lyrics by ROBERT LOPEZ
and JEFF MARX

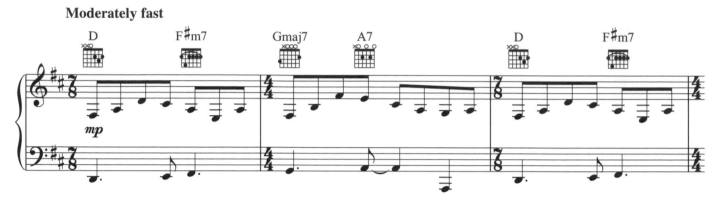

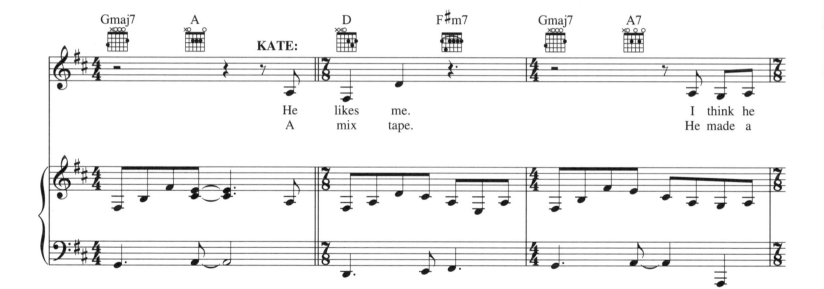

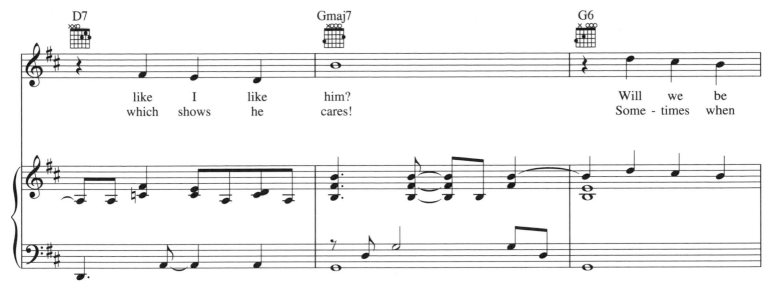

D7   Gmaj7   G6

like I like him?
which shows he cares!

Will we be
Some - times when

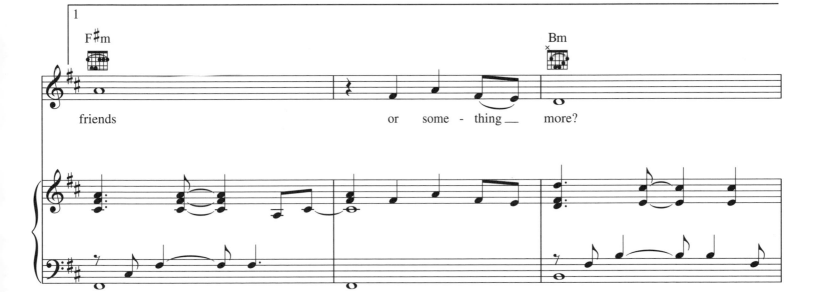

1

F#m   Bm

friends   or some - thing ___ more?

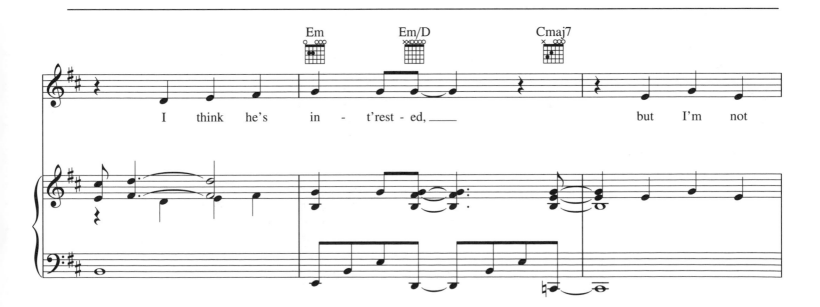

Em   Em/D   Cmaj7

I think he's in - t'rest - ed, ___   but I'm not

Freely

KATE: *Oh... great!*

"I Am the Wal - rus," "Fat - Bot - tomed Girls," ___
"Through _ the Years," ___ **P:** "The Theme from *Cheers*," _

Tempo I

"Yel - low Sub - ma - rine?" _____ What does this mean? _____
KATE: "Mov - ing Right _ A - long." _

Princeton, thank you for this tape! I was just looking at side A. Great songs!

subito **p**

PRINCETON: *Did you get to side B yet? Check it out!*

Nice tape. PRINCETON: *There's one more: "I* Have to Say I Love

You in a Song."

KATE: *He likes me!*

I'M NOT WEARING UNDERWEAR TODAY

from the Broadway Musical AVENUE Q

Music and Lyrics by ROBERT LOPEZ
and JEFF MARX

For more info about *Avenue Q*, visit **www.AvenueQ.com**

SPECIAL
from the Broadway Musical AVENUE Q

Music and Lyrics by ROBERT LOPEZ
and JEFF MARX

LUCY THE SLUT:
I can make you feel spe - cial ___ when it sucks to be you. Let me make you feel spe - cial ___ for an hour ___ or two. ___ Your

For more info about *Avenue Q*, visit www.AvenueQ.com

life's a rou-tine that re-peats each day. ___ No one cares who you are ___

or what you say. ___ And some-times you feel like you're no-bod-y, _____ but

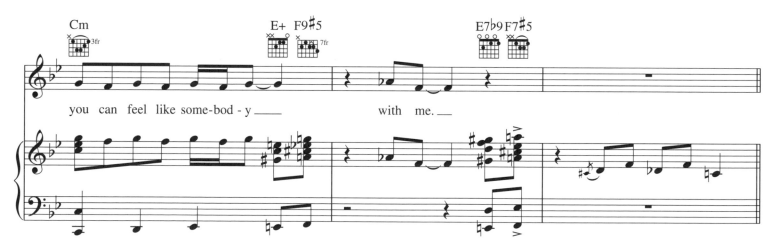

you can feel like some-bod-y ___ with me. ___

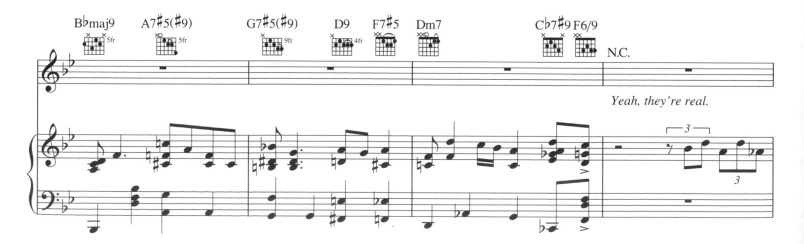

Yeah, they're real.

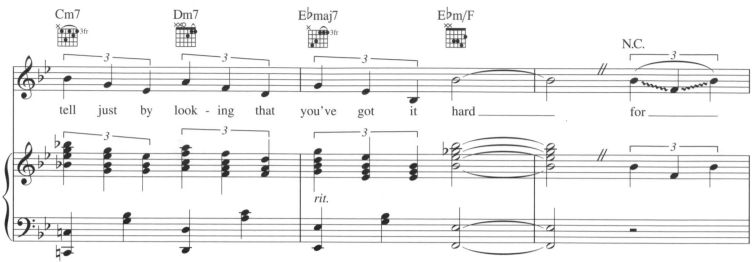

tell just by look-ing that you've got it hard_____ for_____

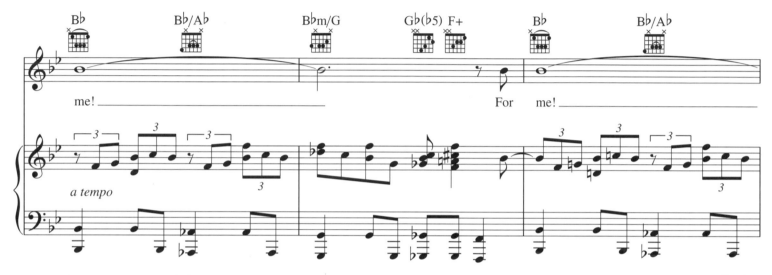

me! _____ For me! _____

_____ For me! For me! For me! For me! I can

tell just by look-in' that you are es-pe-cial-ly hard for me! _____

YOU CAN BE AS LOUD AS THE HELL YOU WANT

(When You're Makin' Love)

from the Broadway Musical AVENUE Q

Music and Lyrics by ROBERT LOPEZ
and JEFF MARX

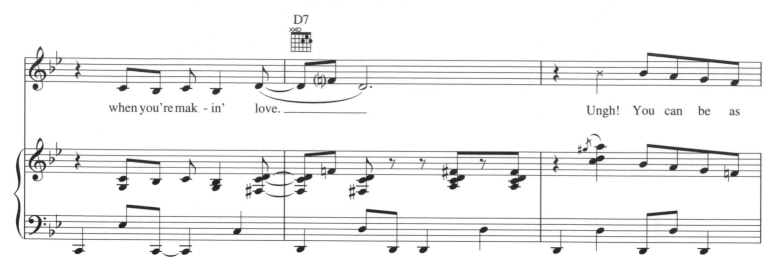

when you're mak-in' love. _____ Ungh! You can be as

loud as the hell you want __ when you're mak-in' love. __

You can be as loud as the hell you wan - TUH!

You're not al - lowed to be loud at the li - brar - y, ___ at the

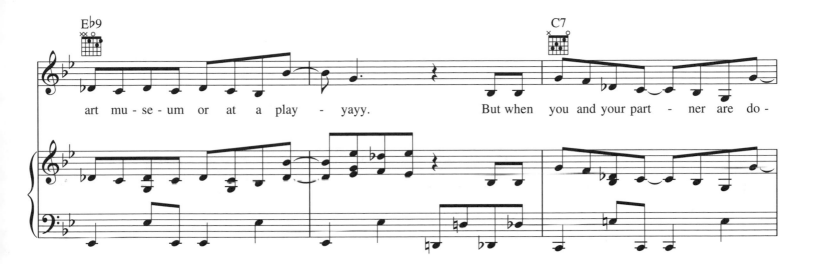

art mu - se - um or at a play - yayy. But when you and your part - ner are do -

- in' the nas - ty, don't be - have like you're at the bal - let! 'Cause you can be as

loud as the hell you ___ want ___ when you're mak - in' love. ___ *Ooh!*

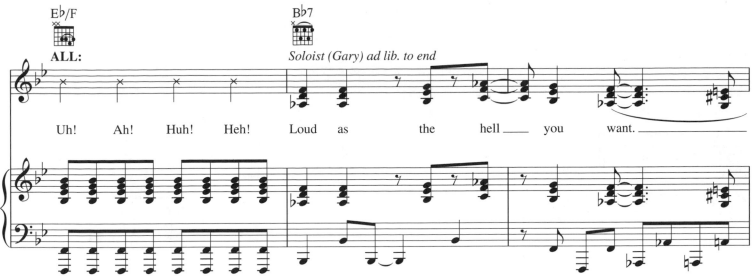

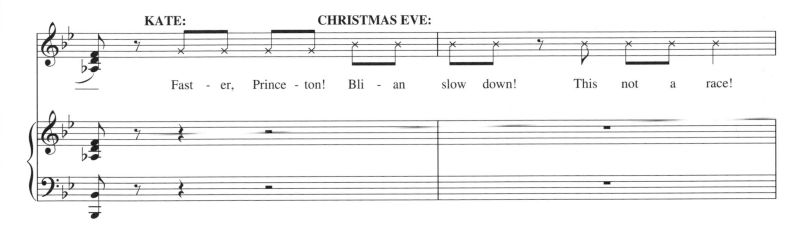

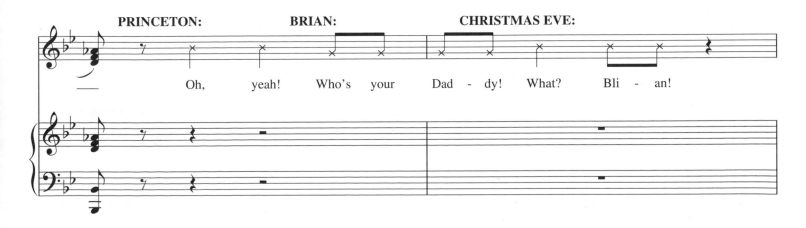

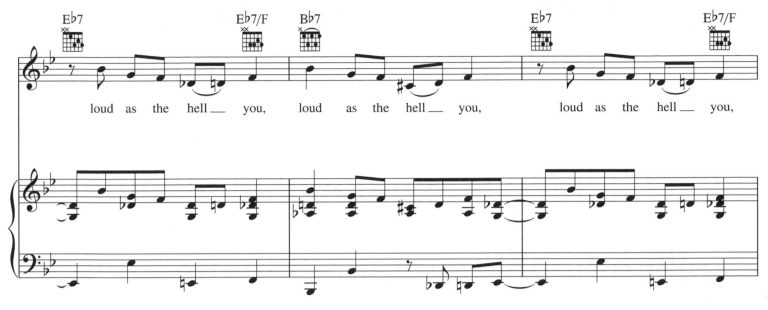

loud as the hell — you, loud as the hell — you, loud as the hell — you,

loud as the hell — you, loud as the hell — you, loud as the hell — you,

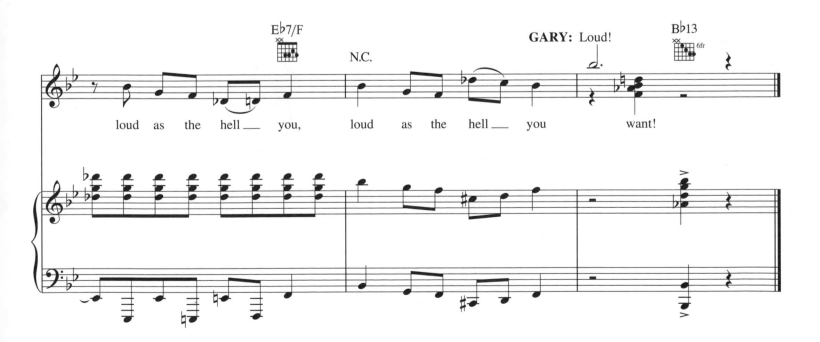

loud as the hell — you, loud as the hell — you want!

GARY: Loud!

FANTASIES COME TRUE

from the Broadway Musical AVENUE Q

Music and Lyrics by ROBERT LOPEZ
and JEFF MARX

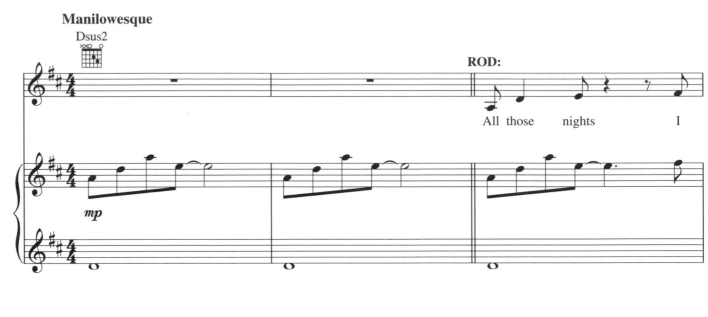

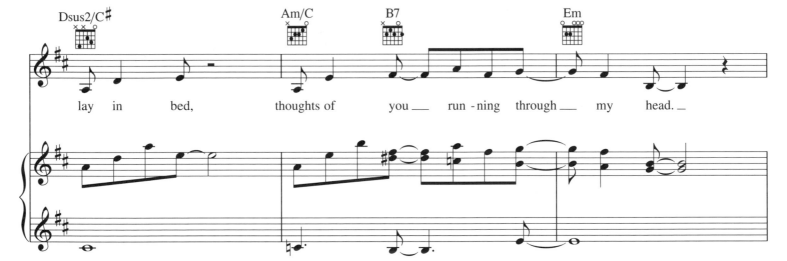

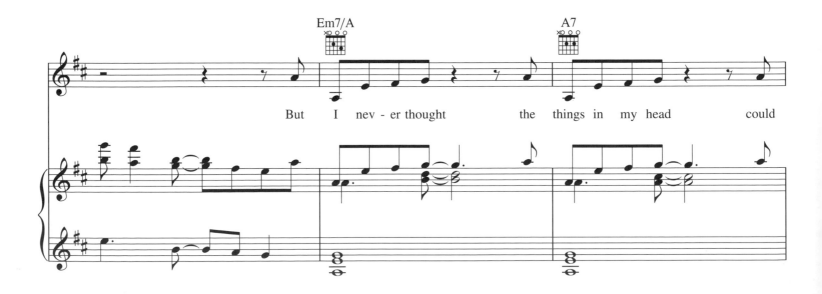

For more info about *Avenue Q*, visit **www.AvenueQ.com**

what was al - ways in __ my mind ___ was in your mind too. __

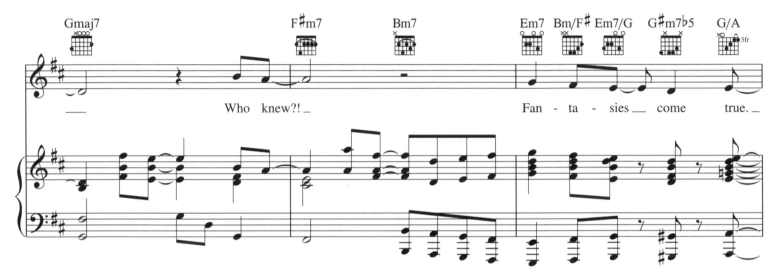

Who knew?! __ Fan - ta - sies __ come true. __

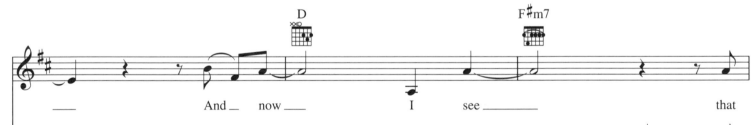

And __ now ___ I see _____ that

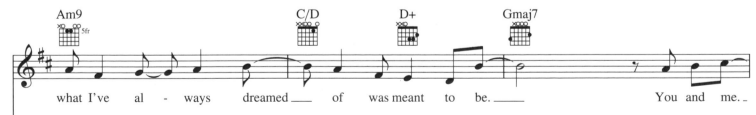

what I've al - ways dreamed ___ of was meant to be. ___ You and me. __

Me — and you. Fan - ta - sies — come

Dream Sequence

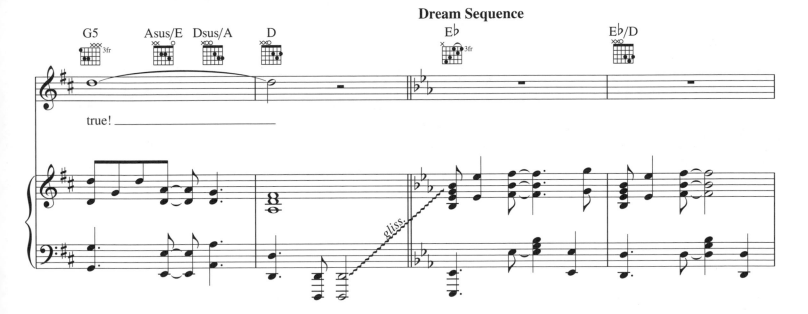

true! _____

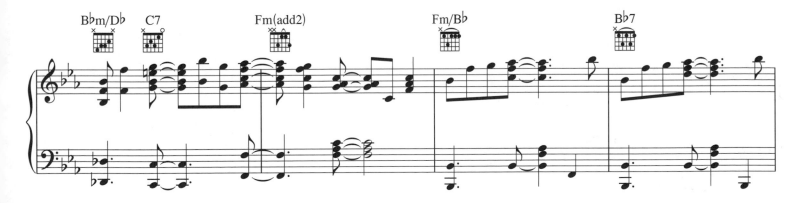

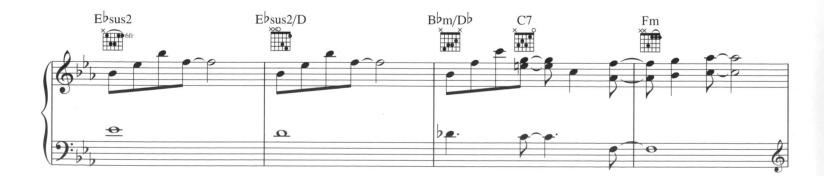

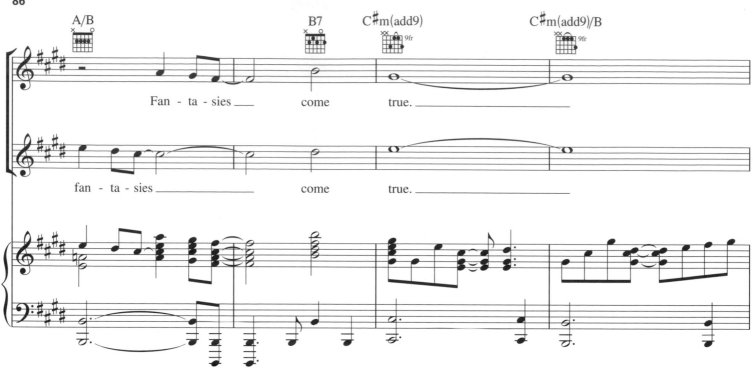

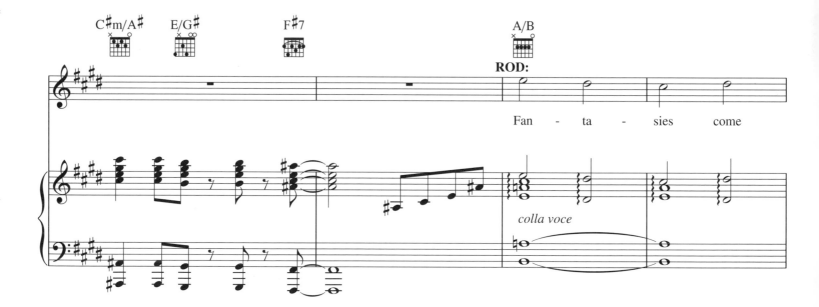

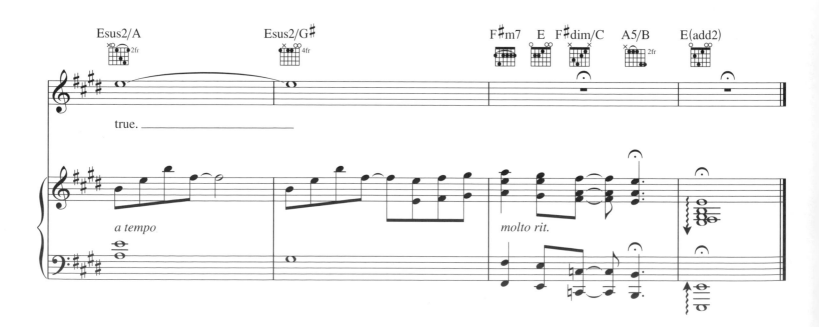

MY GIRLFRIEND, WHO LIVES IN CANADA

from the Broadway Musical AVENUE Q

Music and Lyrics by ROBERT LOPEZ
and JEFF MARX

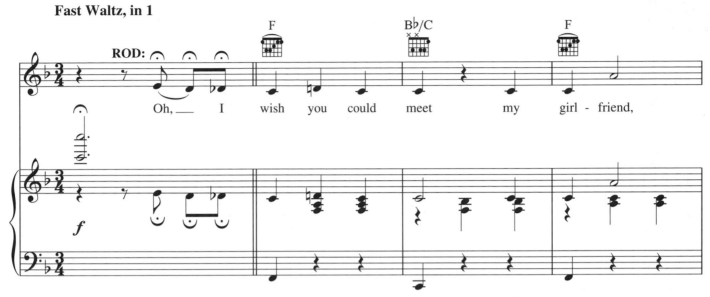

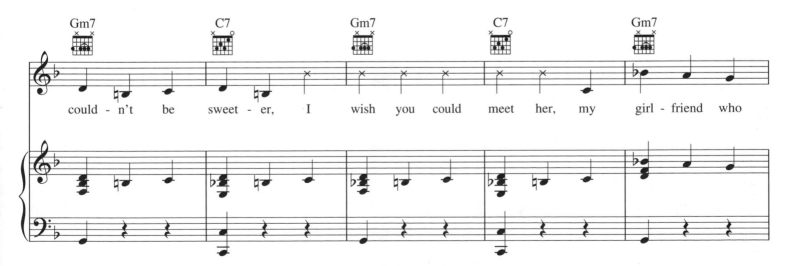

For more info about *Avenue Q*, visit www.AvenueQ.com

lives in Can - a - da! _____ Her

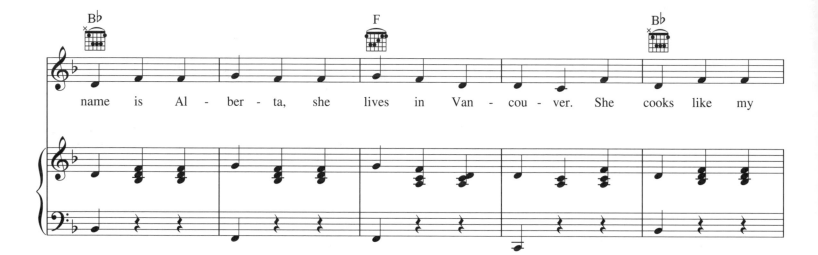

name is Al - ber - ta, she lives in Van - cou - ver. She cooks like my

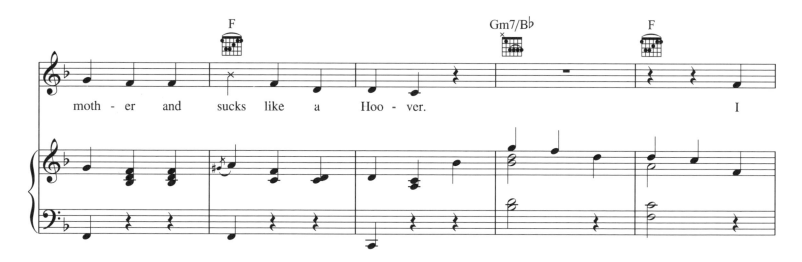

moth - er and sucks like a Hoo - ver. I

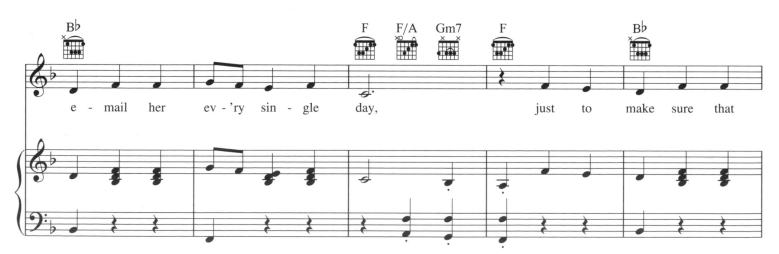

e - mail her ev - 'ry sin - gle day, just to make sure that

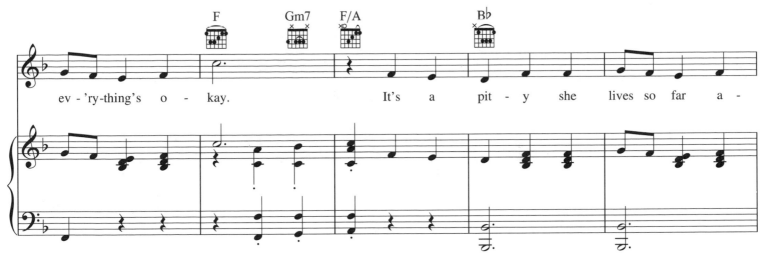

ev - 'ry-thing's o - kay. It's a pit - y she lives so far a-

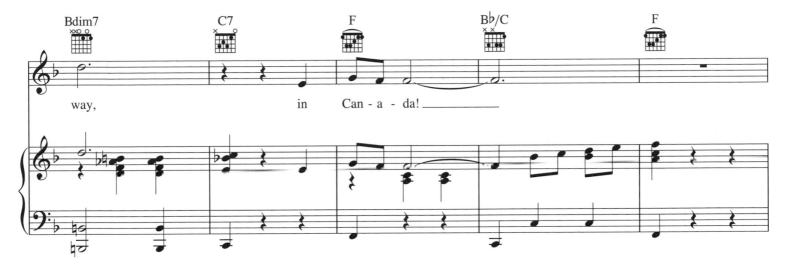

way, in Can - a - da!

Last week she was

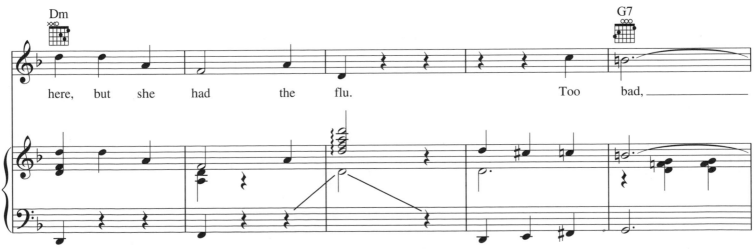

here, but she had the flu. Too bad,

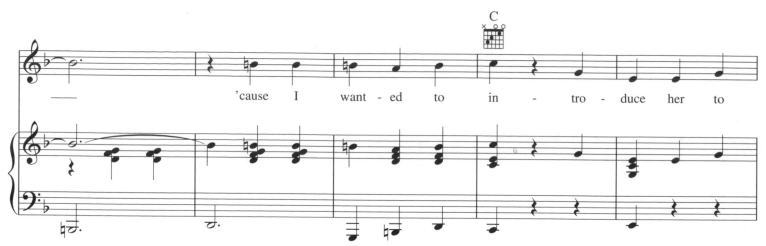

'cause I want - ed to in - tro - duce her to

you. It's so sad, there

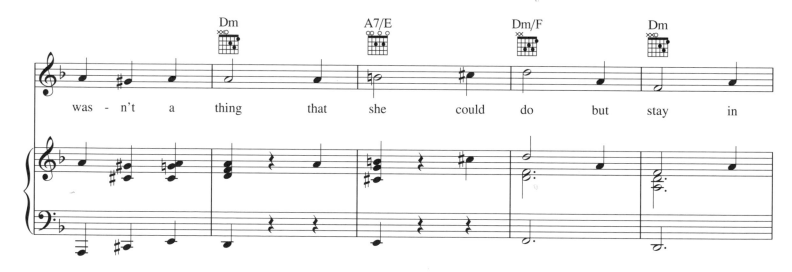

was - n't a thing that she could do but stay in

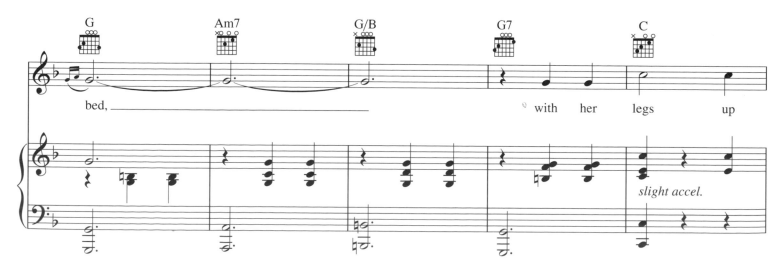

bed, with her legs up

slight accel.

Faster

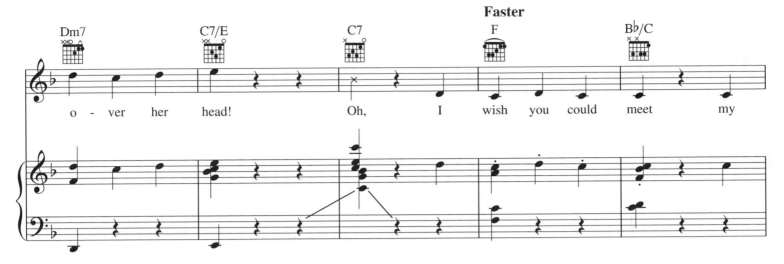

o - ver her head! Oh, I wish you could meet my

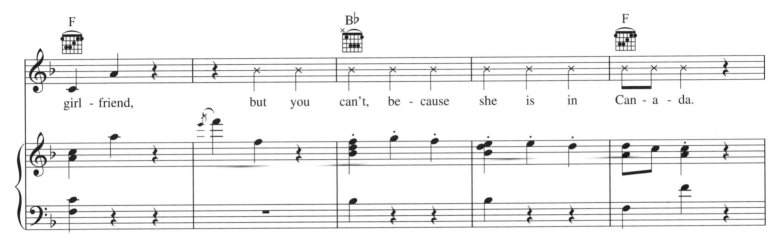

girl - friend, but you can't, be - cause she is in Can - a - da.

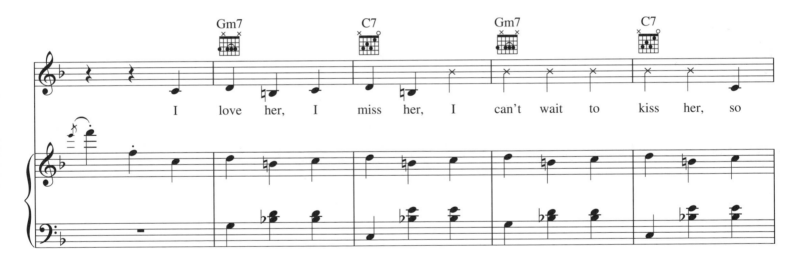

I love her, I miss her, I can't wait to kiss her, so

soon I'll be off to Al - ber - ta! I mean, Van -

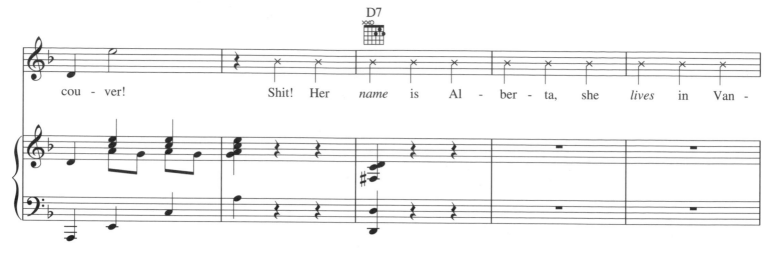

cou - ver! Shit! Her *name* is Al - ber - ta, she *lives* in Van -

cou— ...She's my girl - friend! _ My won - der - ful

girl - friend! _ Yes, I have a girl - friend _ who lives in

Can - a - da! _____ *And I can't wait to* (uncomfortable
eat her pussy again! silence)

THERE'S A FINE, FINE LINE

from the Broadway Musical AVENUE Q

Music and Lyrics by ROBERT LOPEZ
and JEFF MARX

Moderate Folk Rock

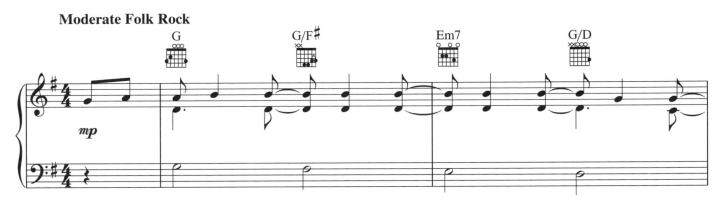

KATE:
There's a fine, fine line ___

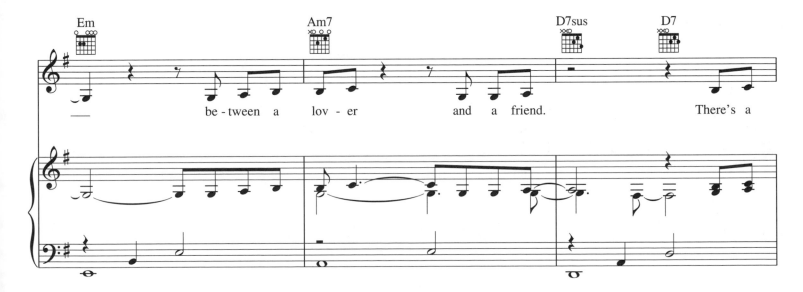

___ be-tween a lov-er and a friend. There's a

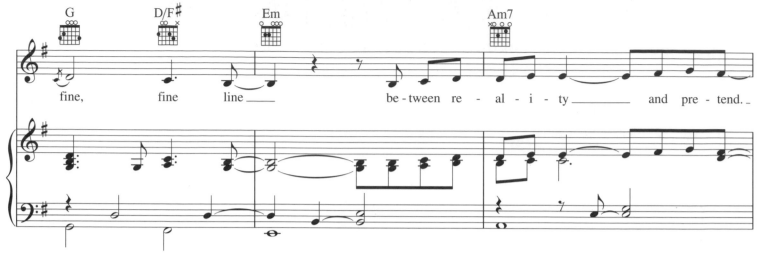

fine, fine line _____ be-tween re - al - i - ty _____ and pre - tend. _

_____ And you nev-er know _ till you reach _ the top _ if it was

worth the up - hill climb. _____ There's a fine, fine line _

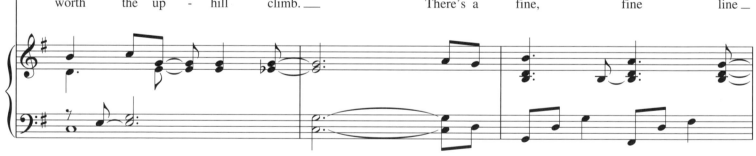

_____ be - tween _ love _____ and a waste _ of _____

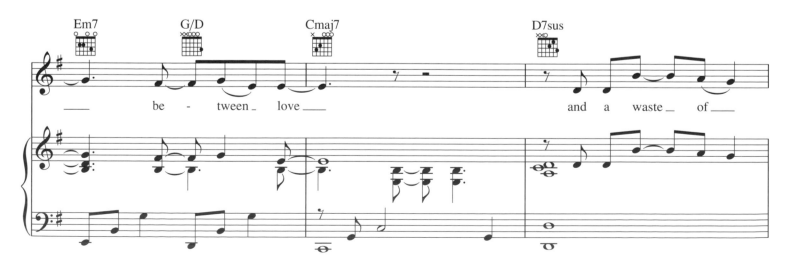

is - n't such __ a crime, __ but there's a fine, fine line __

__ be - tween love __ and a waste __ of your __

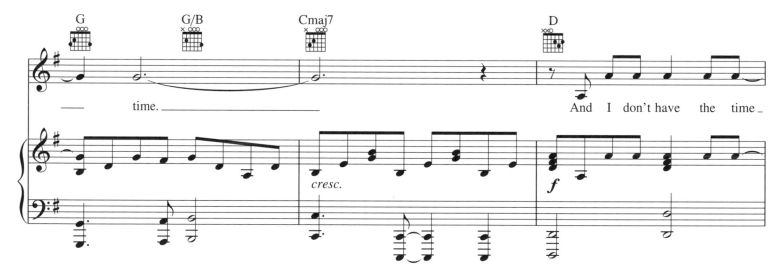

__ time. _____ And I don't have the time __

cresc.

f

__ to waste __ on you __ an - y - more. __

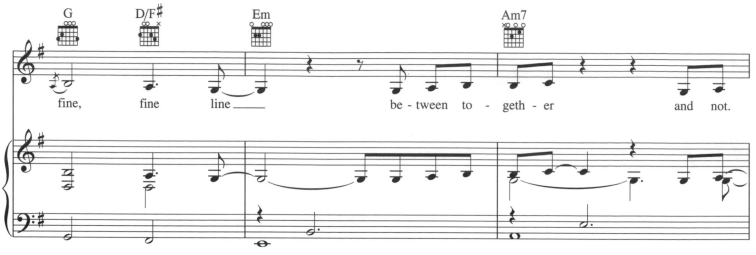

fine, fine line _____ be - tween to - geth - er and not.

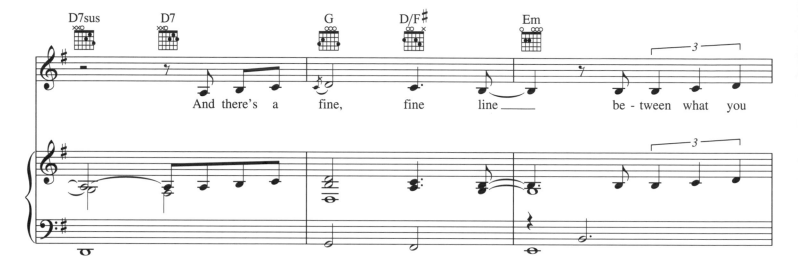

And there's a fine, fine line _____ be - tween what you

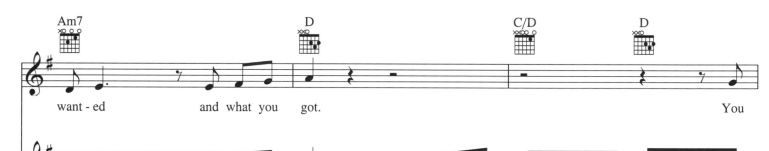

want - ed and what you got. You

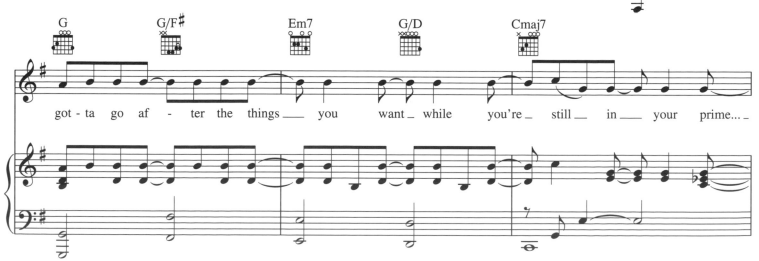

got - ta go af - ter the things _____ you want _ while you're _ still _ in _ your prime... _

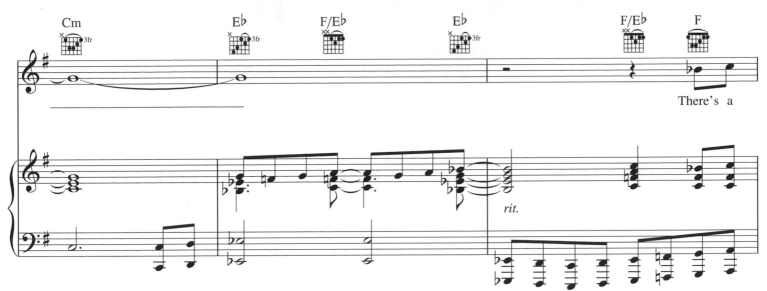

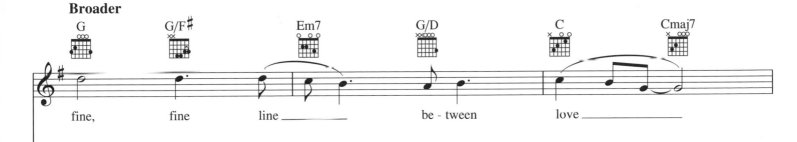

Broader

fine, fine line _____ be-tween love _____

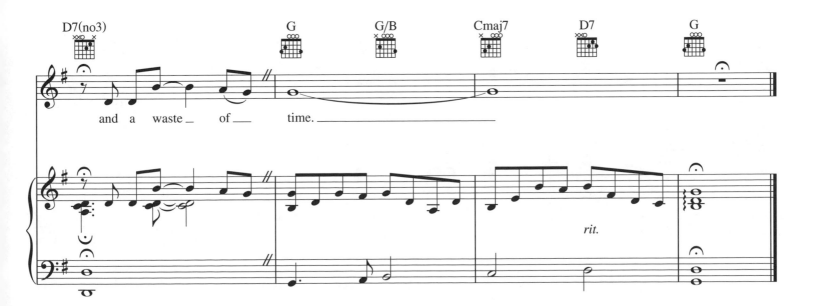

and a waste _ of _ time. _____

THERE IS LIFE OUTSIDE YOUR APARTMENT

from the Broadway Musical AVENUE Q

Music and Lyrics by ROBERT LOPEZ
and JEFF MARX

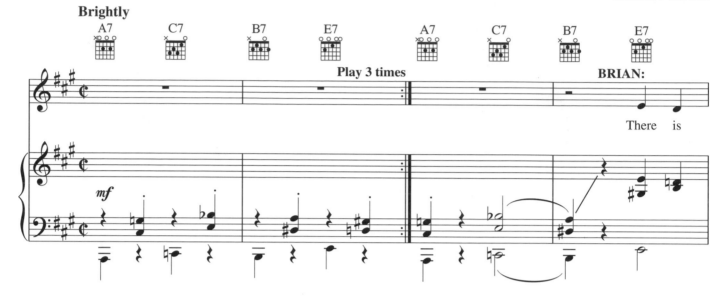

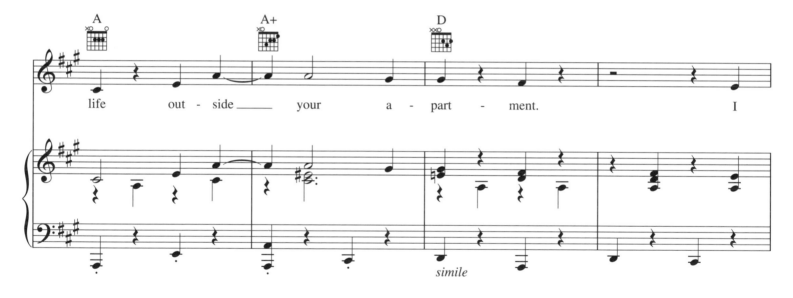

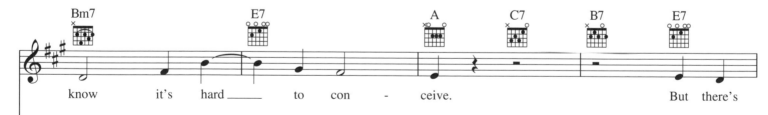

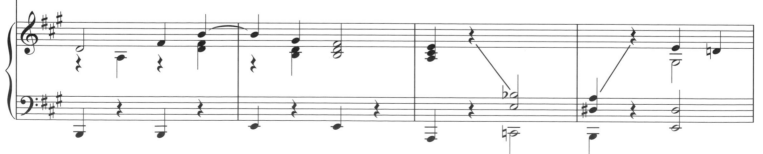

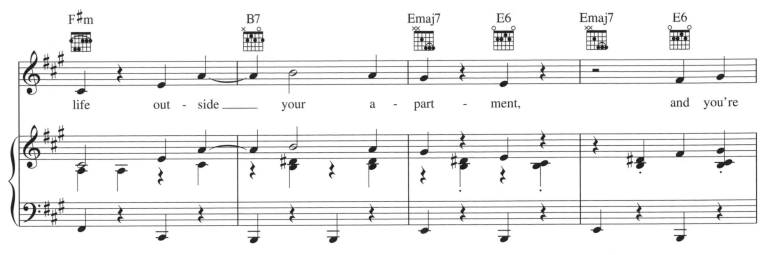

life out - side _____ your a - part - ment, and you're

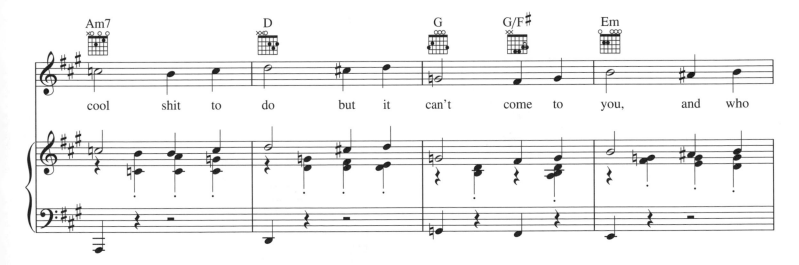

on - ly gon - na see it if you leave. There is

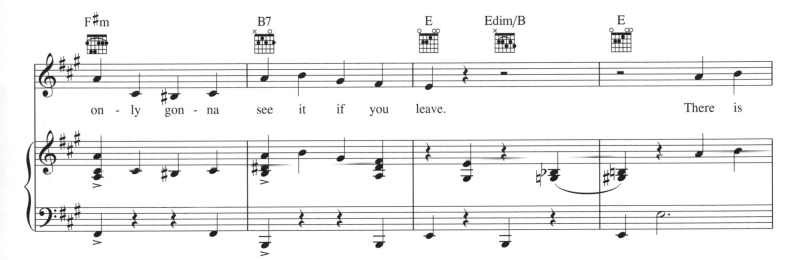

cool shit to do but it can't come to you, and who

knows, dude, you might e - ven score! There is

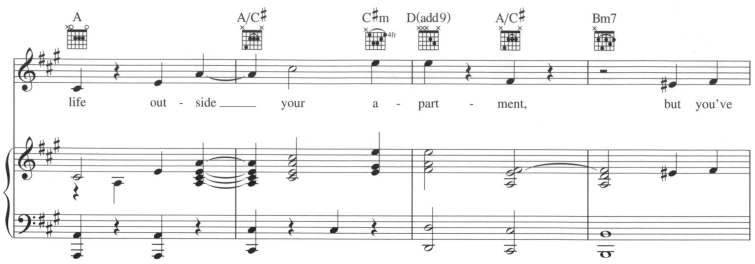

life out - side _____ your a - part - ment, but you've

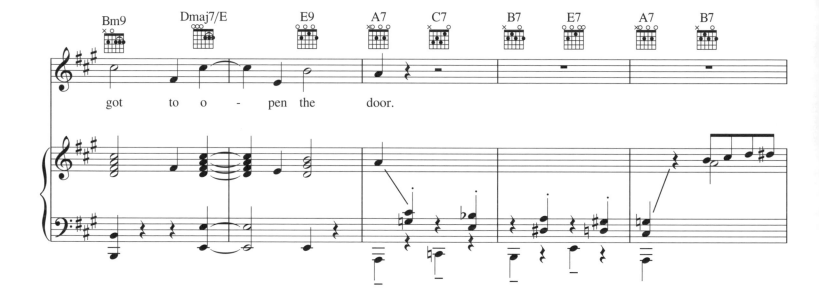

got to o - pen the door.

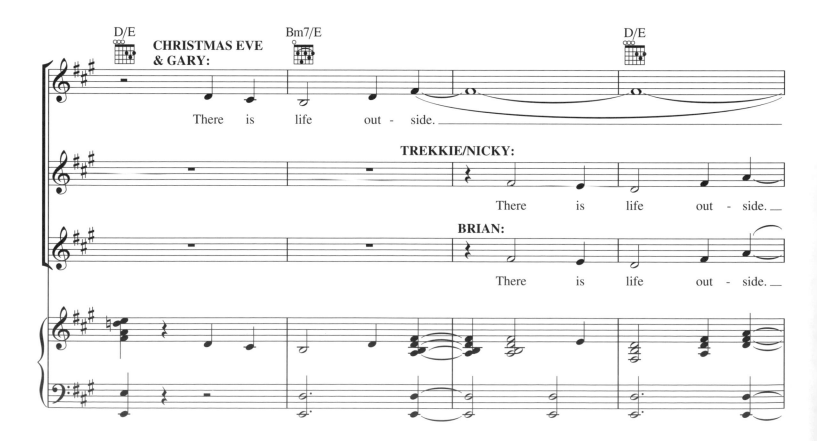

CHRISTMAS EVE & GARY:

There is life out - side. _____

TREKKIE/NICKY:

There is life out - side. __

BRIAN:

There is life out - side. __

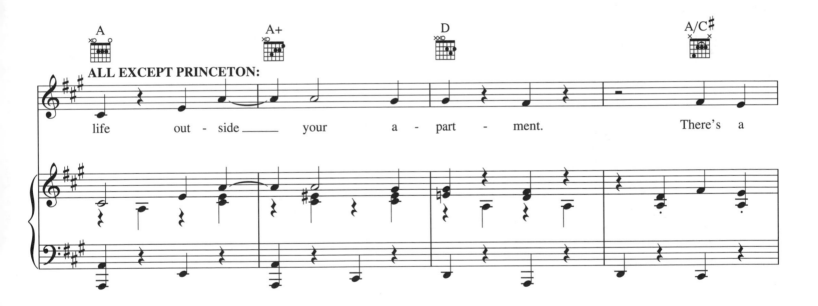

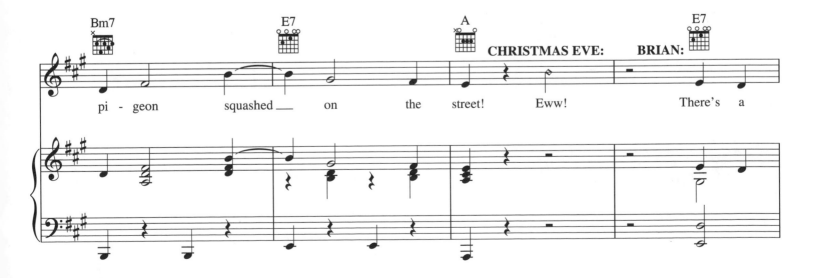

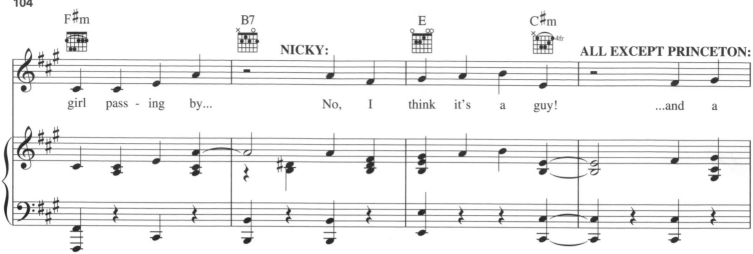

girl pass-ing by... **NICKY:** No, I think it's a guy! **ALL EXCEPT PRINCETON:** ...and a

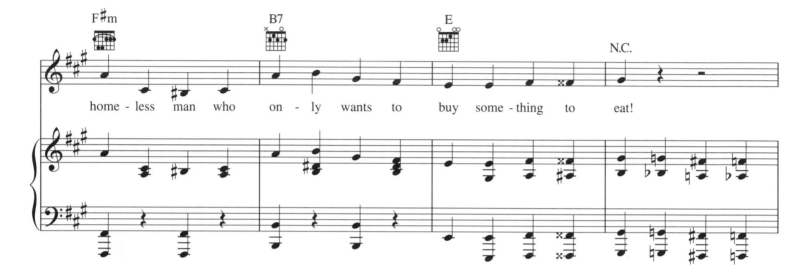

home-less man who on-ly wants to buy some-thing to eat!

Sor-ry. Can't help you. **ALL:** We could

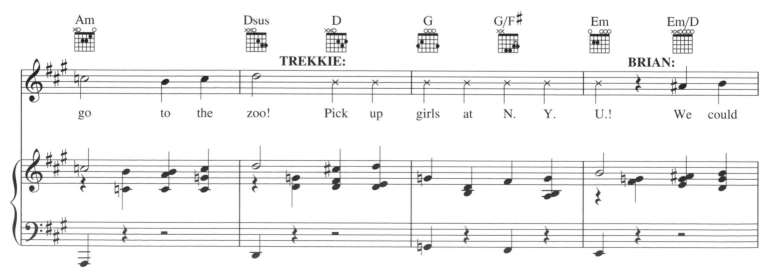

TREKKIE: go to the zoo! Pick up girls at N. Y. U.! **BRIAN:** We could

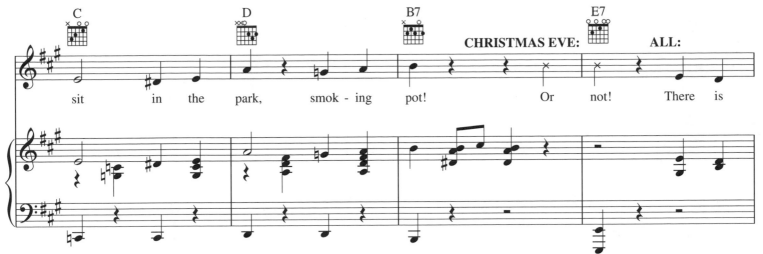

CHRISTMAS EVE: ALL:

sit in the park, smok-ing pot! Or not! There is

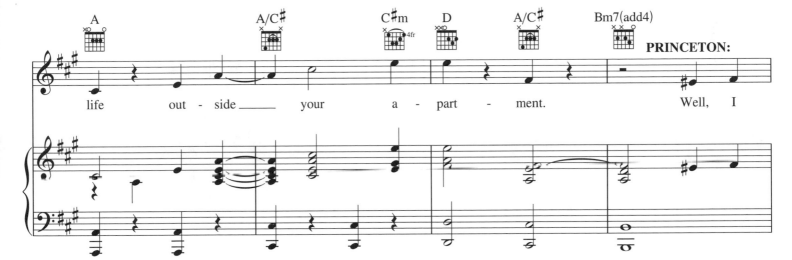

PRINCETON:

life out-side _____ your a-part-ment. Well, I

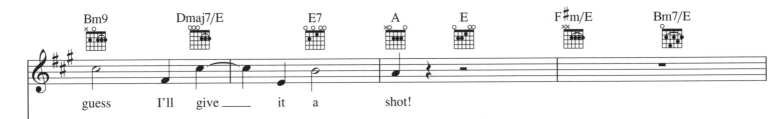

guess I'll give _____ it a shot!

ALL:

There is life out-side _____ your a-

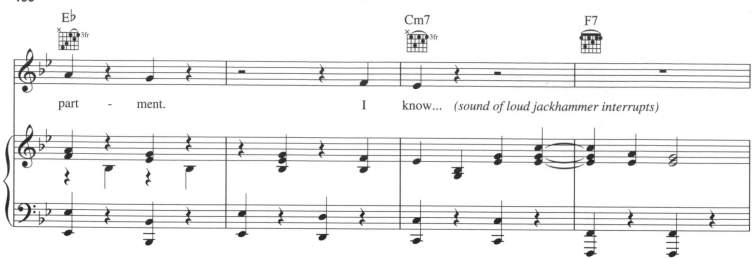

part - ment.   I know... *(sound of loud jackhammer interrupts)*

@&%*!   There is life out - side _____ your a -

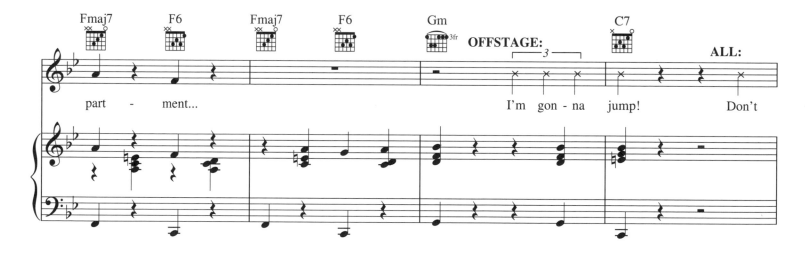

part - ment...   I'm gon - na jump!   Don't

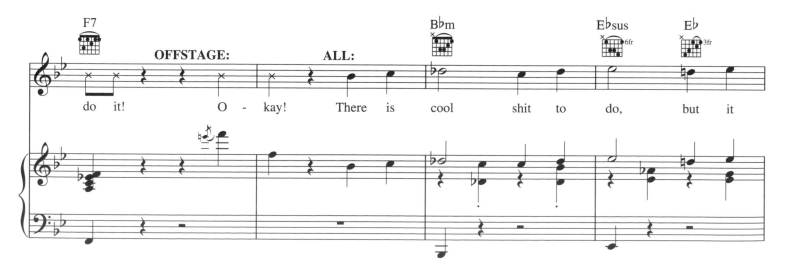

do it!   O - kay!   There is cool shit to do, but it

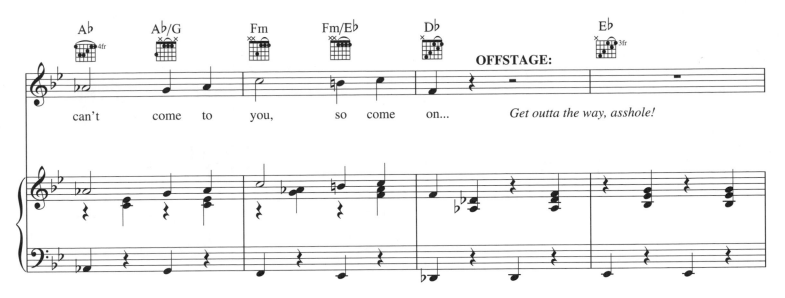

can't come to you, so come on... *Get outta the way, asshole!*

OFFSTAGE:

PRINCETON: *Fuck you!* ALL: There is life out - side _____ your a -

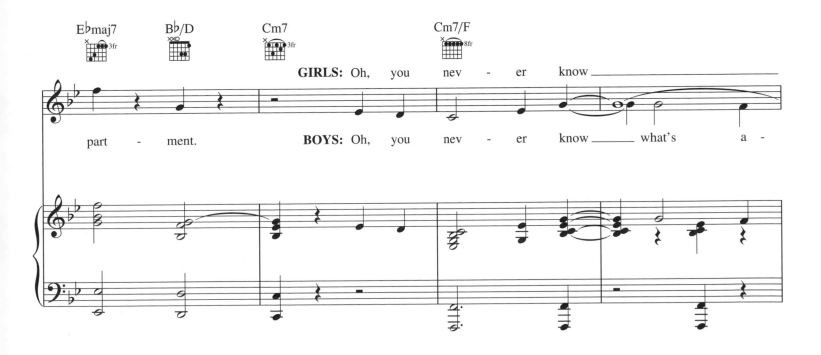

part - ment. BOYS: Oh, you nev - er know _____ what's a -

GIRLS: Oh, you nev - er know _____

You could win the lot - to, or
round the bend.

make a friend!
make a friend!

F7sus   F#7sus   N.C.

GARY/NICKY/TREKKIE/BRIAN:

(Lucy the Slut enters) Take her

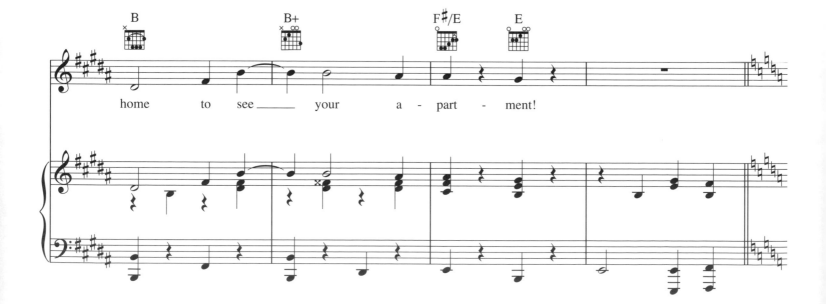

home to see your a - part - ment!

B   B+   F#/E   E

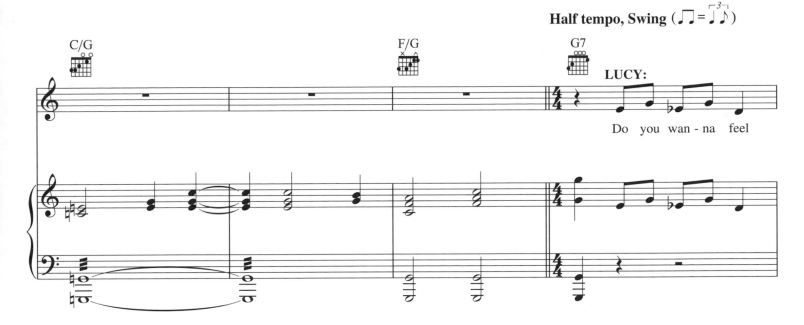

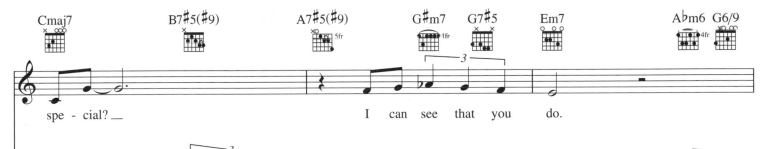

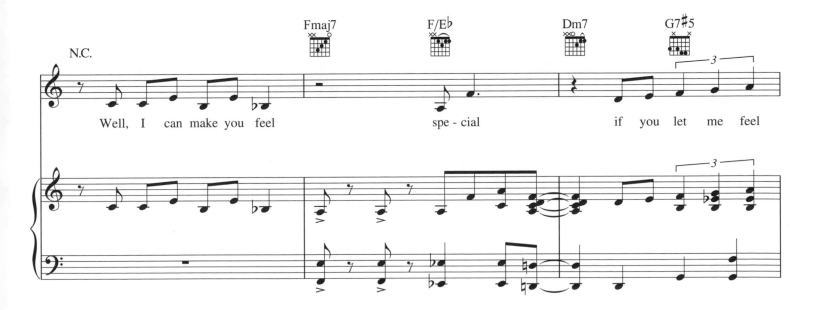

A tempo (♩ = ♩)

Cmaj9   Gm7/C   C   Fm

PRINCETON:

you. _____ Where's your pad? Not too

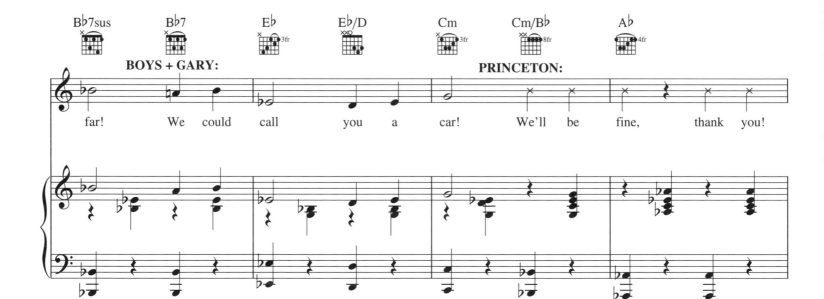

Bb7sus   Bb7   Eb   Eb/D   Cm   Cm/Bb   Ab

BOYS + GARY: **PRINCETON:**

far! We could call you a car! We'll be fine, thank you!

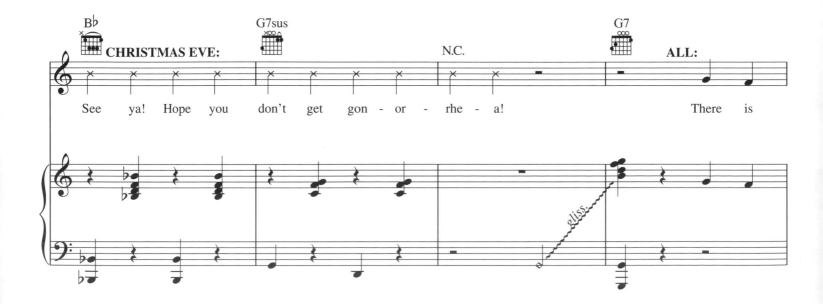

Bb   G7sus   G7

CHRISTMAS EVE: N.C.   **ALL:**

See ya! Hope you don't get gon - or - rhe - a! There is

life out - side _____ your a - part - ment! _____

LUCY &
PRINCETON: But now it's time to go home!

GARY, BRIAN,
CHRISTMAS EVE: There is life out - side _____ your a -

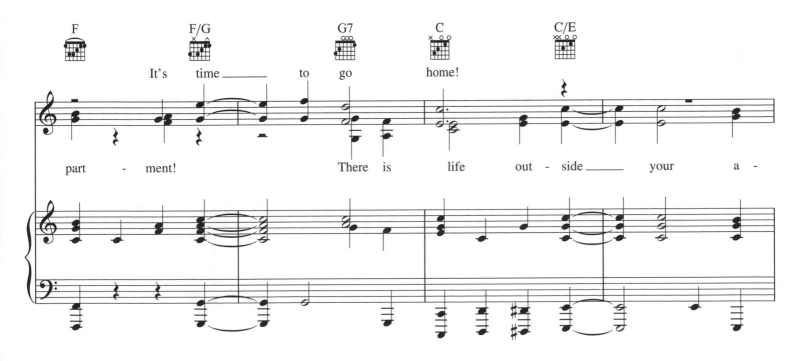

It's time _____ to go home!

part - ment! There is life out - side _____ your a -

It's time to go home!

part - ment! There is life out - side

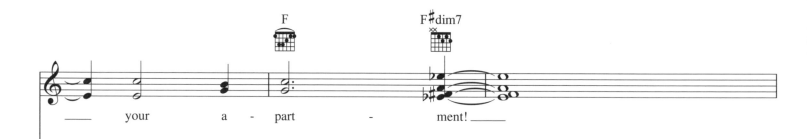

your a - part - ment!

ALL: But now it's time to go home! **TREKKIE:** For porn!

THE MORE YOU RUV SOMEONE

from the Broadway Musical AVENUE Q

Music and Lyrics by ROBERT LOPEZ
and JEFF MARX

* *The character of Christmas Eve is Japanese-born and speaks with a thick accent, which has been approximated with phonetic spellings. The composers offer their sincere apologies to those who may be offended.*

tly for mak - ing peace with them and ruv - ing, that's why you

ruv so strong you rike to make him die. The more you

A tempo (flowing)

ruv some - one, the more he make you cla - zy. The more you

ruv some-one, the more you wish-ing him dead. Some-time you

rook at him and on-ry see fat and ra - zy, and want-ing

base - bar bat for hit-ting him on his head!

poco rit.

ruv, he ar - so bling-ing sol - lows. The more you

Tempo I

ruv some - one, the more you want to kir - rem. _____

Ruv - ving and kir - ring fit rike hand in gruv! So if there

some - one you are want - ing so to kir - rem, you go and

find him, and you get him and you no kir - rem. 'Cause chanc - es

good he is your ruv. _____

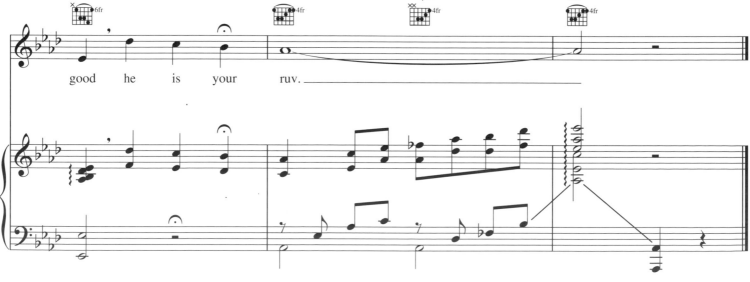

SCHADENFREUDE

from the Broadway Musical AVENUE Q

Music and Lyrics by ROBERT LOPEZ
and JEFF MARX

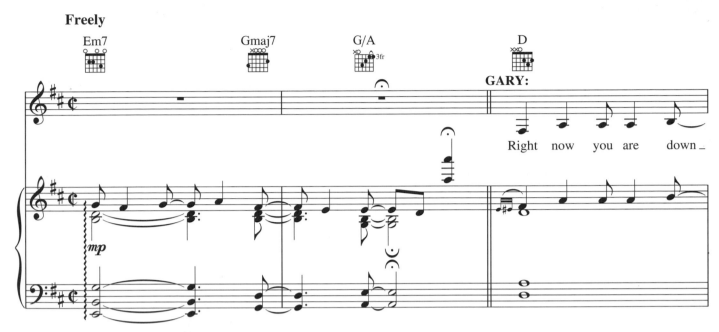

GARY:

Right now you are down

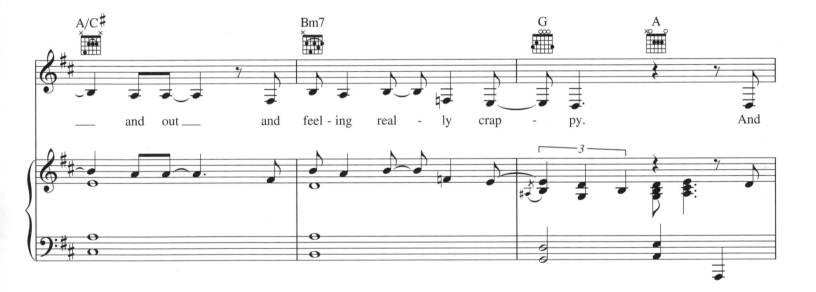

and out and feel-ing real-ly crap-py. And

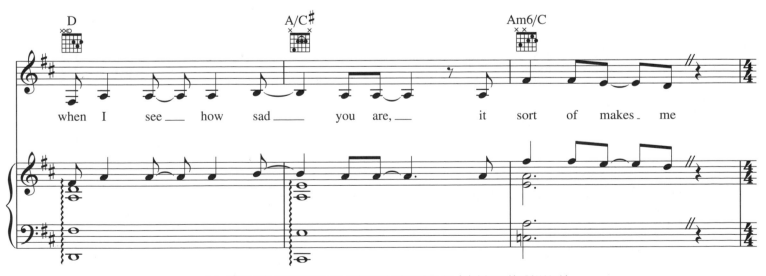

when I see how sad you are, it sort of makes me

Moderate Rock

hap - py! *Happy?* NICKY: GARY: Sor - ry Nick - y, hu -

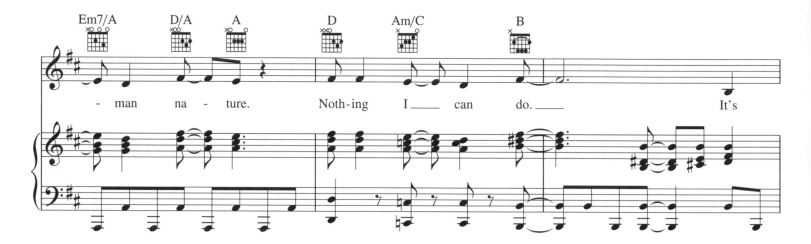

- man na - ture. Noth-ing I ___ can do. ___ It's

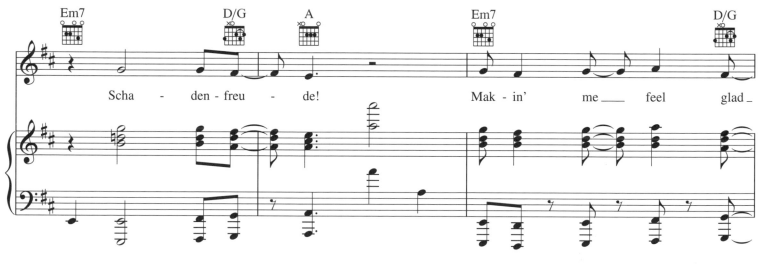

Scha - den-freu - de! Mak - in' me ___ feel glad ___

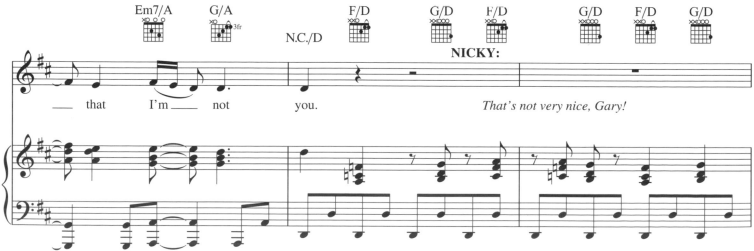

___ that I'm ___ not you. *That's not very nice, Gary!*

I didn't say it was nice, but everybody does it.

GARY:

D'ja ev-er clap when a wait-

-ress falls _____ and drops a tray _ of glass - es? _____ And

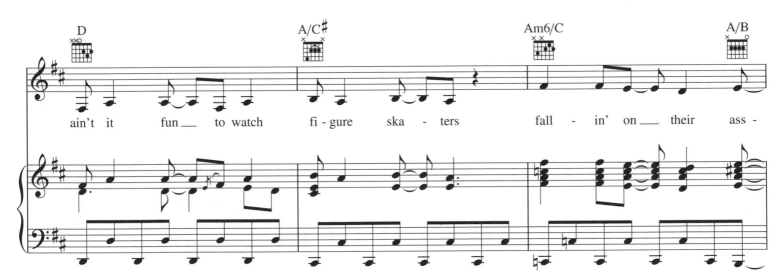

ain't it fun _ to watch fi - gure ska - ters fall - in' on _ their ass -

-es? _____ Don't ya feel _ all warm _ and co - zy,

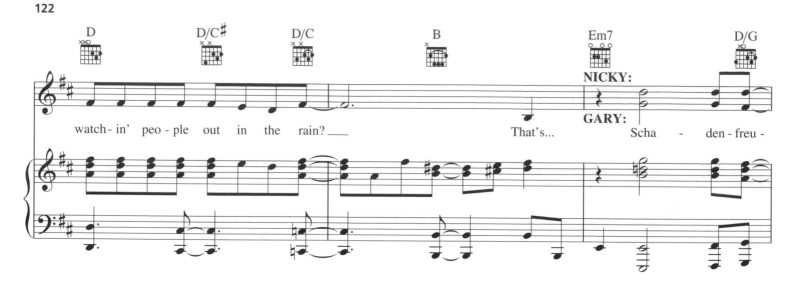

watch-in' peo-ple out in the rain? ___ That's... **NICKY:** **GARY:** Scha - den-freu-

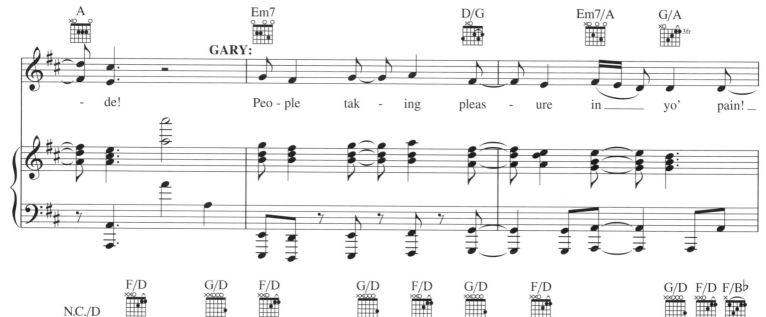

GARY:

- de! Peo - ple tak - ing pleas - ure in ___ yo' pain! ___

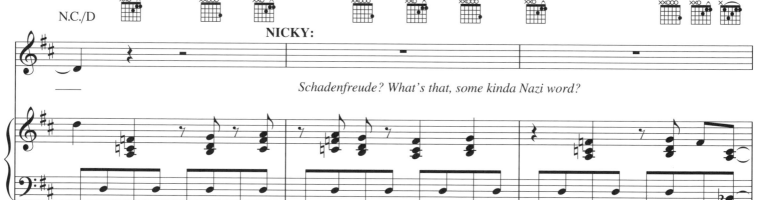

NICKY:

Schadenfreude? What's that, some kinda Nazi word?

GARY: **NICKY:**

Yup! It's German for "Happiness at the misfortune of others!" *"Happiness at the misfortune of others?" That is German!*

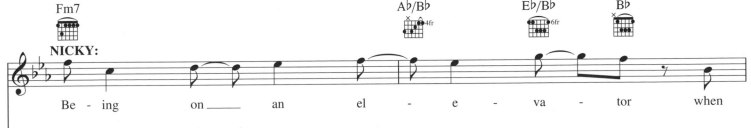

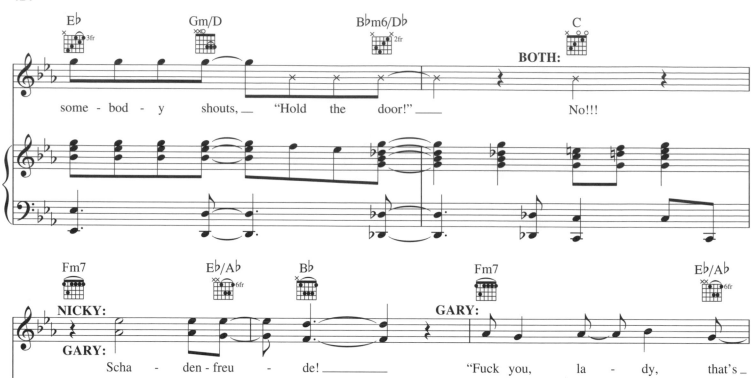

some-bod-y shouts, __ "Hold the door!" __ No!!!

NICKY:
GARY:
Scha - den-freu - de! _____ "Fuck you, la - dy, that's _

__ what stairs _ are for!" __

NICKY:
Ooh, how about

straight "A" stu - dents get - ting "B"'s!   Ex - 's get - ting S. T. D.'s!

don't want to be us, and that makes them ___ feel great. ___

NICKY:

___ We pro-vide ___ a vi - tal serv - ice

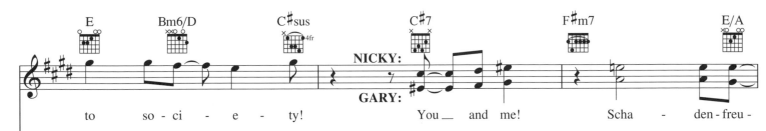

NICKY:

GARY:

to so - ci - e - ty! You ___ and me! Scha - den - freu -

- de! ___ Mak-ing the world ___ a bet - ter place... ___

Mak-ing the world ___ a bet-ter place... _____

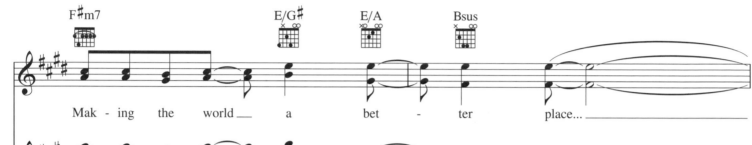

Mak-ing the world ___ a bet-ter place... _____

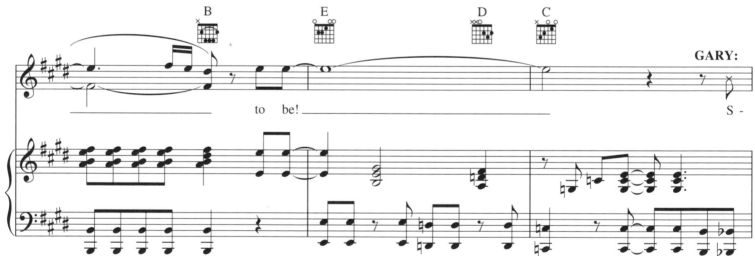

_____ to be! _____

GARY:

S-

C-H-A-D-E-N-F-R-E-U-D-E!

I WISH I COULD GO BACK TO COLLEGE

from the Broadway Musical AVENUE Q

Music and Lyrics by ROBERT LOPEZ
and JEFF MARX

For more info about *Avenue Q*, visit www.AvenueQ.com

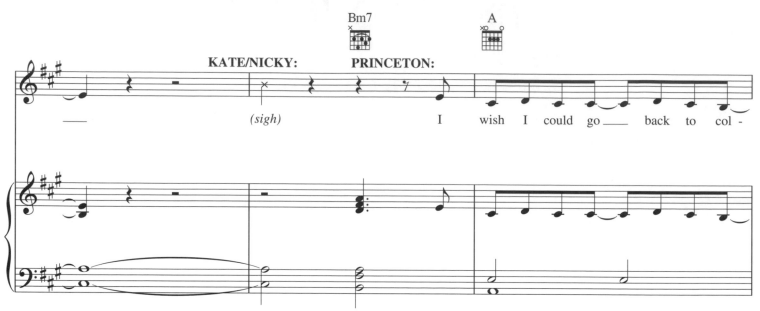

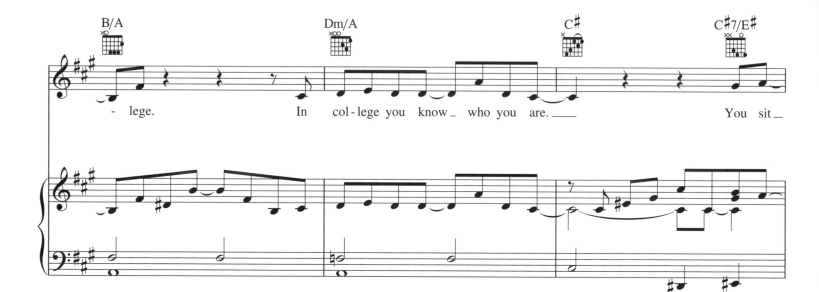

How do I go ___ back to col - lege? I don't know ___

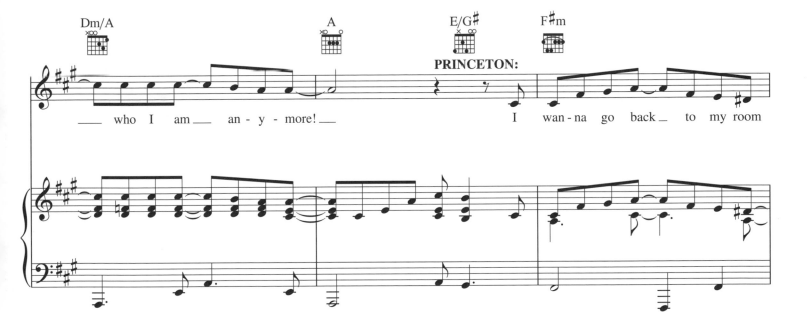

___ who I am ___ an - y - more! ___ I wan - na go back ___ to my room

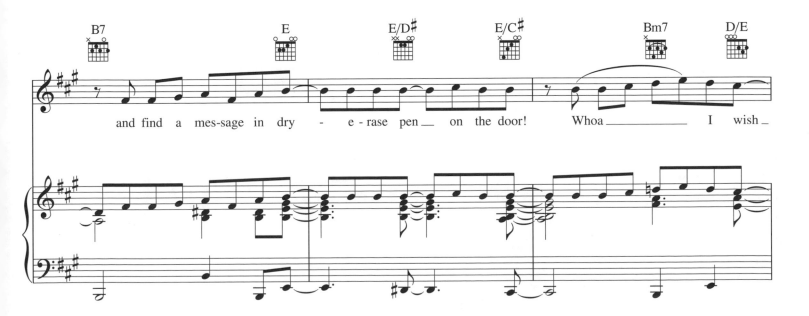

and find a mes-sage in dry - e -rase pen ___ on the door! Whoa ___ I wish ___

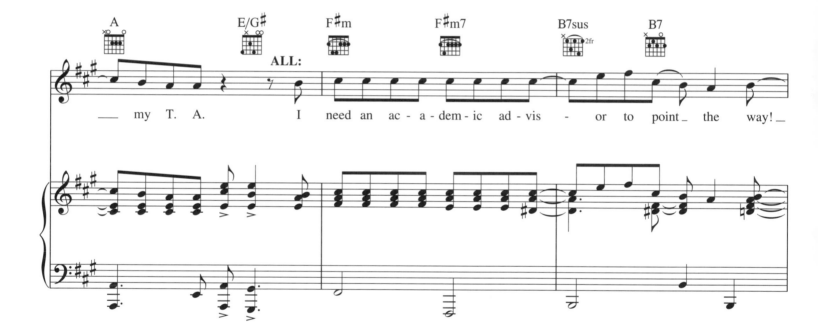

-ter lab, ___ four A. M. be-fore a fi-nal pa-per is due, ___

curs-ing the world ___ 'cause I did - n't start soon - er, and

see-ing the rest ___ of the class ___ there, too! ___

PRINCETON:

I

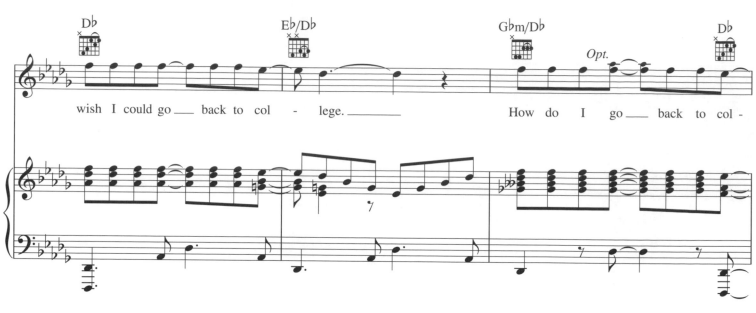

wish I could go ___ back to col - lege. ___ How do I go ___ back to col-

- lege? ___ **KATE:** Ah! ___ **PRINCETON:** I wish ___

N&P: Ah! ___

___ I had tak - en more pic - tures. But, if I were to go ___ back to col-

NICKY:

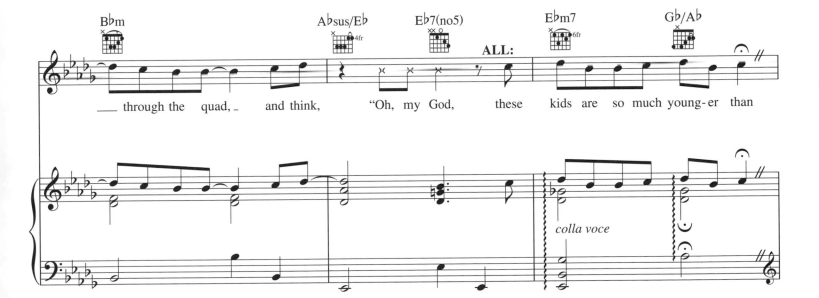

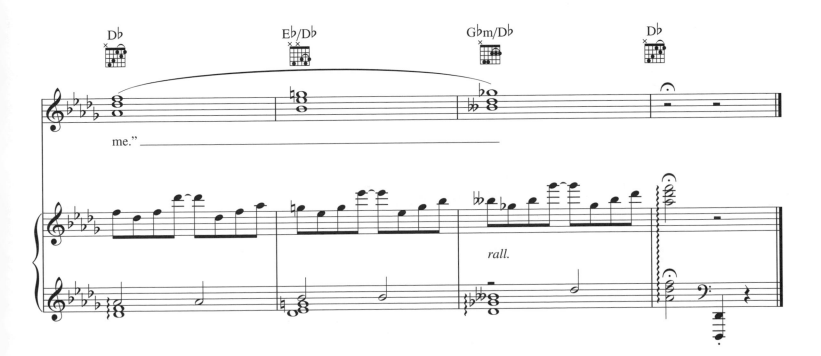

THE MONEY SONG
from the Broadway Musical AVENUE Q

Music and Lyrics by ROBERT LOPEZ
and JEFF MARX

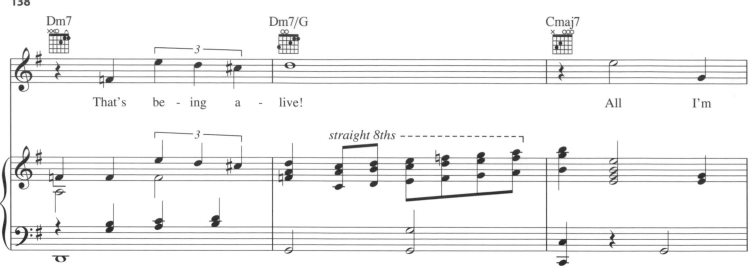

That's be-ing a-live! All I'm

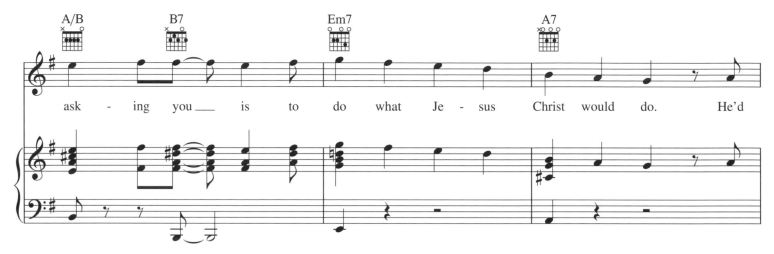

ask-ing you ___ is to do what Je-sus Christ would do. He'd

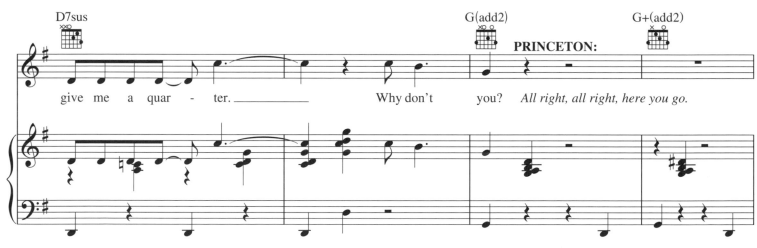

PRINCETON:

give me a quar-ter. ___ Why don't you? *All right, all right, here you go.*

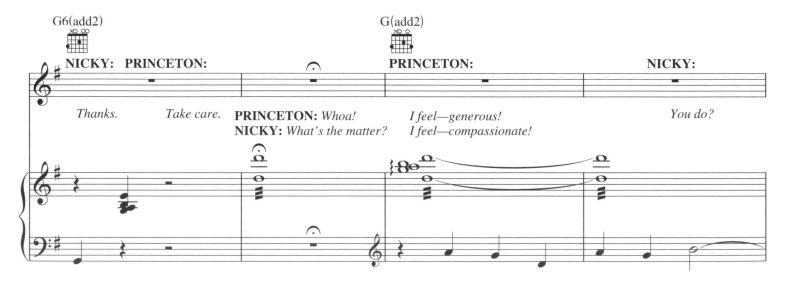

NICKY: PRINCETON: **PRINCETON:** **NICKY:**

Thanks. *Take care.* **PRINCETON:** *Whoa!* *I feel—generous!* *You do?*
NICKY: *What's the matter?* *I feel—compassionate!*

Slower, dreamy

...I can't! I need it! I'm homeless!
I can't! I need it! I'm homeless!
I can't! I need it! I'm homeless!
(Princeton slaps Nicky)

NICKY: *I'd like to, but I'm homeless!*   **NICKY:** *O.K., here you go.*

NICKY:

Sud-den-ly, I am feel-ing clos-er to God. ____

A tempo

It's time to stop beg - ging. It's time to start giv - ing!

What can I give __ to Rod? *Something he'll like so much he'll take me back...I know! I'll find him a boyfriend!*

Slightly slower; Rock tempo

PRINCETON: *That's the spirit!*

BOTH:

When you __ help oth - ers, _____ you

can't help help-ing your-self! ___

NICKY:

PRINCETON:

When you __ help oth -

* All parts sung where written.

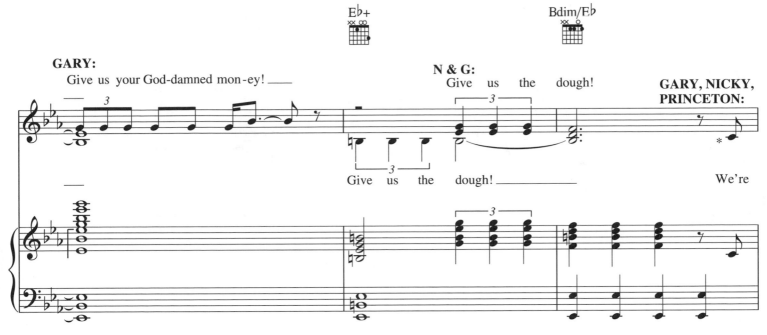

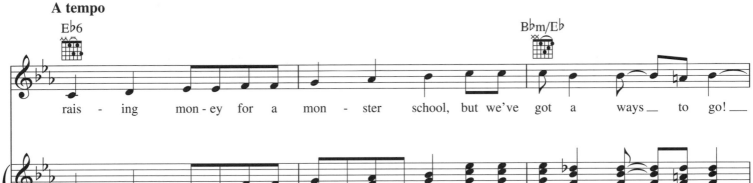

* Gary sings where written. Nicky and Princeton sing an octave lower.

*men sing where written.

FOR NOW

from the Broadway Musical AVENUE Q

Music and Lyrics by ROBERT LOPEZ
and JEFF MARX

CHRISTMAS EVE: You're going to have to make a few com-pro-mis - es, for

TREKKIE MONSTER: ALL:

now, _____ for now. But on - ly for

TOP: CHRISTMAS EVE, GARY*
BOTTOM: NICKY (For now!) ___

ALL OTHERS:

(For now!) ___

now! _____ On - ly for now! _____ On - ly for

*Christmas Eve and Gary sing one octave lower than written.

Christmas Eve and Gary sing one octave lower than written.

**men sing where written*

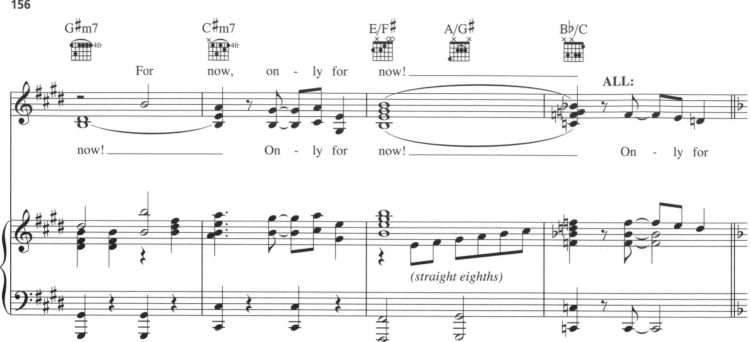

Don't stress, re - lax, let life roll off your backs. Ex -

cept for death and pay - ing tax - es, ev - 'ry - thing in life is on - ly for

poco rall. *rall.*

Slower

NICKY: Each time you smile, __ **KATE:** it - 'll on - ly last a - while. __

now! On - ly for now... on - ly for

PRINCETON: Life may be scar-y, **ALL 3:** but it's on-ly tem-po-ra-ry.

now. On-ly for now. Tem-po-rar-y.

ALL EXCEPT PRINCETON:

Ba-dum - ba-dah, ba-dum - ba-dah, ba-dum ba-dah, da da da da.

da _____ Da da da da da dah dah da.

Da da da da da da da da. _____

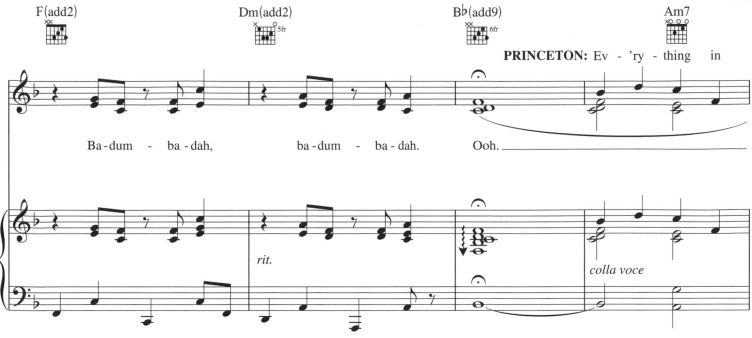

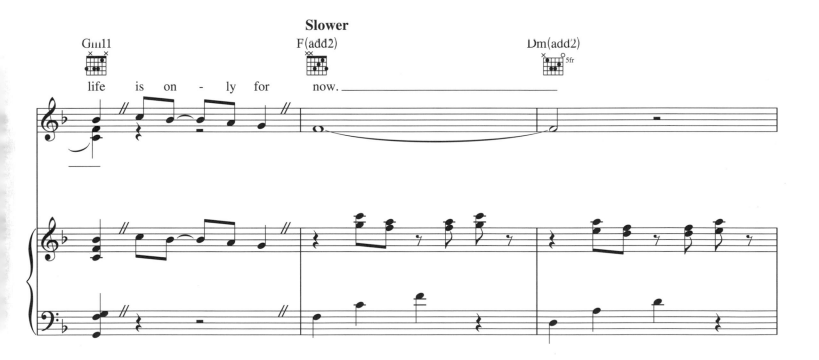

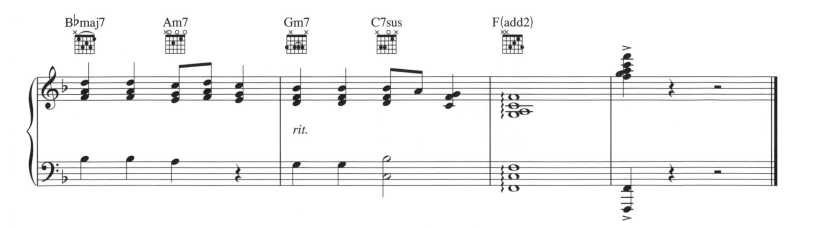